Cost Containment Through Employee Incentives Program

Pat N. Groner

ASPEN SYSTEMS CORPORATION
GERMANTOWN, MARYLAND
1977

658.314
G 87b

"This publication is designed to provide accurate and authoritative information in regard to the Subject Matter covered. It is sold with the understanding that the publisher is not engaged in rendering legal, accounting, or other professional service. If legal advice or other expert assistance is required, the services of a competent professional person should be sought." From a Declaration of Principles jointly adopted by a Committee of the American Bar Association and a Committee of Publishers and Associations.

Dedication

The story that unfolds in this book is a story about people. The program's first appeal is to management, of course; but, as in most things, the real accomplishments came to be because Baptist Hospital of Pensacola, Florida, enjoyed the service of hundreds of hardworking, flexible men and women. From our first day of operation in 1951, they have been *can do* people, capable of accepting change and embracing ideas that were new or progressive.

The setting for the productivity incentives experiment is not a plush, well-endowed institution—quite the contrary. The hospital and its people have had to claw and scratch to overcome financial shortcomings; and, because this has remained a historically consistent truth, management and staff have communicated well on the subject. Perhaps the most outstanding example of this occurred in 1970–71, when the hospital undertook its only capital funds campaign since its opening. In the planning, fund raising advisors urged that initial contacts be made among directors and medical staff, where potentials for success might be greatest. But we as management urged otherwise, looking with greater faith to the employees themselves. And that proved a good decision! As pacesetters, the employees set a standard that challenged all others, and the campaign pushed on to an unprecedented community success. Time after time, these loyal and dedicated people have illustrated their strengths and their belief in "their hospital."

The productivity incentives experience was one more incident in a lengthy chain of successes. Thus it is only fitting that this book—and all that it may imply for the future benefit of the country's health care system—be dedicated to the men and women who work at Pensacola, Florida's Baptist Hospital.

Table of Contents

List of Tables and Figures

Acknowledgments

The saga of productivity incentives, including this volume, is anything but a one-man show. As the narrative describes, the piece-by-piece assembly of the program and its subsequent upgrading to more sophisticated levels have been the product of many persons' thinking. I would like to acknowledge just three:

The first is John H. Schill.

John joined Baptist Hospital in 1956 as an administrative resident and remained until 1970. In most of those years he was assistant administrator. Schill is one of those unique people whose makeup includes many specific management skills but who is also something of a philosopher; he is able to sit back reflectively and see ways to move from the present to the future. More than any other person, he deserves credit for conceiving the initial concepts in the incentive plan; he was the innovator, the salesman, the analyst. Without him, this plan would never have been born. For this and countless other contributions, our hospital owes John Schill a great debt of gratitude.

The second figure is John Appleyard.

John has been Baptist Hospital's "Boswell" for many years, and both this program and this book bear his imprint. From the day the first unit incentive was conceived, his input was present. When it became desirable for us to conduct seminars to explain the plan, he developed the cases and filmed materials on which those programs were based. When I decided to record the hospital's efforts in incentives, he was my collaborator, acting as coauthor for both Parts One and Two and general editor throughout. This book, and a second one recording the twenty-five-year history of the Baptist Hospital, were written simultaneously, indicating John's deep involvement with our institution.

The third is H. James Hicks, Jr.

Hicks is a staff consultant for Medicus Systems Corporation and, as such, joined Baptist Hospital in 1974. A skilled analyst and industrial engineer, he slipped comfortably into our productivity philosophy and was able to use the successes of the past to build for the future in revising our overall incentives engineering. Having done this, Jim Hicks became coauthor of Part Two of this volume.

Preface

When I began my career as hospital executive over a quarter century ago, it was in a health care world that by comparison with the present can only be described as calm and collected. The nation had just emerged from the war, and, though there was a new awareness of the values of hygiene and the physical person, changes came slowly. When I moved to Pensacola in 1950 to preside over the opening of a new hospital, I was literally the entire administrative staff. There were no assistants and few staff specialists other than professional ones. The only government involvement was through a Hill-Burton construction grant. Americans largely believed that those who pursued health careers were "a chosen few"—ones whose calling was almost like the taking of religious orders and should be compensated accordingly. Even so, Baptist Hospital, created after a ten-year struggle by local citizens of good will, had to scratch hard for financial integrity.

I begin this story with that background because all hospital executives —especially the younger ones—must remember that hospitals were not always beset with the tensions, conflicts, and urgency present today. Those responsible for hospitals today face an almost totally new perspective: there is the constant pressure by employees for higher incomes; the public, voicing its newfound consumerism, cries out for better services; the physician and his technically oriented paramedical cousins have regular demands for new equipment at fantastic cost; and government, insurance carriers, and those who pay their own tariff clamor against the upward sweep of hospital charges.

Things were not so twenty-five years ago—or at least so it seemed. In fact, that is part of the reason hospital managers from Maine to California are experiencing trauma in meeting the new expectations.

Historically, emphasis in hospitals was directed to *care*, personalized attention, and compassion in a labor-intensive atmosphere. A quarter century ago, some hospital leaders might have worked by the theory that "the more money we spend the better care we'll deliver". But that philosophy was not readily recognizable.

Today the gentle pace is gone. Those in authority are goaded on all sides by demands, many of which are self-defeating at least, and overwhelming for the voluntary hospital system at worst. Because both "the system" and the social expectations have developed so rapidly, there has been little opportunity to address the financial and motivational mechanics at work. Instead, we are still employing age-old philosophies and theorems, approaching today's multidemands with yesterday's methods.

Only recently have figures of national reputation begun to question that perhaps hospitals are missing the boat by not introducing efficiencies that have made industrial America a world pacesetter: strategies such as mergers, multiinstitutional systems, investor-owned chains, specialty staff (industrial engineers and finance people), continuing education, and a more deliberate corporate structure, to suggest a few.

This book is a true story, a chronicle of our hospital spanning more than a decade, dealing with what we have termed *productivity incentives*. It is not a book on theory. It is a summary of actual experiences, successes, and the failures enjoyed by a hospital that grew from a 300–to a 500–bed acute general hospital while trying to give employees a voice in their earnings, to generate interest among 1,000 persons in "minding the store" where supply usage is concerned, and to develop a new sense of personal responsibility for operating costs through a sharing of savings between the employee AND the patient.

The story also encompasses recognition that no such system, even one proven successful, can be static. The chapters will relate the problems encountered in meeting enquiries raised by governmental agencies, tax officials, insurance companies, and others, while management utilized the skills of outside specialists to give a working program continuing success.

It is hoped that the results will prove even to conservative Doubting Thomases that this concept, installed in hospitals with the proper environment, created by managements dedicated to higher salaries, lower charges, and improved quality, *can* result in multidigit savings year after year for patient and taxpayer, with higher earnings for hospital employees and finer service in the bargain.

That satisfies just about everyone, doesn't it? Now, if all this has piqued your curiosity, let's begin.

Introduction

Some sage once said that success was an idea whose time has come.

That is how I regard this book. Actually, I toyed with producing it for six or seven years. Yet, there was always either something more pressing to do or some tactical reason that suggested that the book's time had not come.

Now, however, the time seems right.

To those who know me or who have heard one of the talks I have made on this subject, the topic of Productivity Incentives (or rather, the program at Pensacola, Florida's, Baptist Hospital) will not be totally new. What *is* new is the fact that there is a decade of data on which to base conclusions. Some information is highly positive; other factors are less so, but their very existence helps support the contention that an incentive plan, soundly conceived and strongly administered, can be an important factor in the nation's quest to provide quality health care with price responsibility.

As the reader will see, Baptist Hospital's program was filled with good and bad news. When administration was able to focus appropriate attention on the subject matter and the supervision of details, results proved outstanding. As long as the program functioned according to plan, the hospital, its staff, and its patients profited in terms of thousands of annual benefit dollars. When staff ability to manage the program slipped, the tempo suffered accordingly. However, even in later years when the departure of a key man, a major construction program, and interference from the Internal Revenue Service temporarily interrupted a smooth plan flow, the good results of prior years continued. Once the habits of watchfulness and thrift were established, they were largely maintained. Even during inflation, the hospital continued to build cost differentials between its statistics and those of comparable institutions to the benefit of the entire community.

In the following chapters, I attempt to tell it all; the mistakes are noted as well as, with equal care, the principles.

Equally important, I hope you will recognize the timeliness of the subject.

When Baptist Hospital introduced its incentives plan, the institution was something of a voice in the wilderness. Many hospital officials did not believe that such a philosophy was appropriate for health care organizations. They were backed up by a century of experience in which health care organizations rejected management science almost *in toto*. But now, in the mid-1970s, the shape of things is changing. Hospitals and members of government are coming to recognize the need for efficiencies that could—if properly promoted—substantially reduce the nation's health care bill. In the past there was actually a negative government incentive for hospitals to be efficient. As this attitude changes, the role of the quality productivity incentive is going to loom large.

This book follows a somewhat unusual course. Following these brief introductory remarks are illustrations of how we proceeded and our results, followed by plans being made for future improvement, and then supportive data.

One other point: up to this writing, incentive programs have been something of an academic exercise in the nation's hospitals. As you will see in a later chapter, Baptist's management hosted a number of visits by other administrative leaders, and several copied the methods after attending workshops. Other visitors came, too, specialists whose backgrounds related to this area of management expertise. Among them was the late Dr. J. J. Jehring, who for many years headed the prestigious University of Wisconsin Center for the Study of Productivity Motivation. Dr. Jehring spent weeks reviewing the program and talking with participants. His findings, later recorded in his book, *The Use of Subsystem Incentives in Hospitals,* strongly supported the incentives method. So did a study by a team from the American Hospital Association's Hospital Research and Educational Trust, whose members surveyed innovative programs in ten hospitals nationwide. Their findings were reported as Innovative Hospital Management Programs: A Summary of Ten Case Studies. There were other analyses, too, including complimentary studies and reports by Abt Associates, commissioned by the Department of Health, Education, and Welfare, and by Roy Littlejohn Associates, Inc., as a result of work by the National Commission on Productivity.

But all the studies, reports, and records are part of the past. Now our hospital is looking to something more scientific, substantial, fundamental, and far-reaching. With the help of specialists from the Medicus Systems Corporation, methods have been revamped, placing new stress on quality as well as productivity. Formulas, which are the program foundation, have been reengineered. As the times beckon, I believe the hospital is ready for a new era.

Part One

Part One

Chapter 1

In the Beginning

Baptist is typical of hundreds of other U.S. hospitals. It opened in 1951 with 95 beds, enjoyed modest success, and expanded twice prior to 1963. In that year, another physical enlargement began, bringing capacity to roughly 325 beds.

From the beginning, the hospital's management had to scratch for money and, since operating capital structure was weak, the board had to innovate. Also, Pensacola, Florida, is a community with a conservative local power structure. Three fund-raising campaigns raised $600,000, a substantial portion of the original building capital, and that effort gave citizens a keen sense of participation with the institution. The hospital board, in turn, felt (and still feels) a strong community oriented obligation to offer topflight care at charge levels as low as possible.

INCENTIVES TOWARD COST CONTROL

To remain solvent, the management zeroed in on cost controls. The word "incentive" was part of the hospital's initial operating vocabulary. For example: the sick leave program was designed as an incentive; the retirement plan was written to include incentive features; and a suggestions plan has a high benefit scale. From its inception, management utilized frequent hospitalwide employee meetings to communicate, keeping personnel appraised of plans and needs. Praise was given when possible, but we "told it like it was" when things were difficult. The result was an enduring close-knit family atmosphere in which people trust one another and share the pride of accomplishment. Part of this feeling stems from early emphasis on principles which foster the good of the group. Sick leave is one example.

3

THE SICK LEAVE EXAMPLE

Traditional sick leave programs evolve into incentives to be dishonest. They establish numbers of days off per year, and administrative practice actually encourages people to *use* the time, whether they are ill or not. Countless employers thus build a needless cost into operations, encouraging absenteeism without providing the real protection such a program should, in our opinion, be designed to create.

Baptist Hospital built its plan the other way. At the beginning, the plan paid for no sick time until the employee had been away from the job for five days; then it provided half pay. The current deductible period is two days.

The plan has a sliding benefits scale that grows in coverage with length of service. After one year, the employee is protected for ten weeks of sick leave; after three years, for thirty weeks. The scale moves upward —after seven years of service one is guaranteed sick time for fifty weeks.

The plan provides unprecedented security, yet its cost to the hospital is borne by savings realized from the control on short term illnesses. This approach concentrates resources to benefit the longer service staff member when he or she needs help most.

Admittedly, some younger service employees are critical of the plan. They see people in other organizations cashing in on those extra little vacations; but our long service people, the backbone of the hospital, applaud the plan. Once an organization has had a few lengthy cases and the word gets around, thinking people realize that this plan is an incentive both to the individual and to management: our plan is many thousands of dollars per year less costly than conventional ones, a saving that helps keep charges low.

An additional advantage to this philosophy has been its effect on controlling absenteeism. We have almost none of the costly, time consuming one- and two-day absences. Where some plans make it easy for personnel to take advantage of marginal situations to miss work, ours does not. We believe this encourages basic honesty. We want to help the employee who should be away from the job due to illness or injury; we do *not* want to encourage him to take advantage of such leave unfairly.

SHORTENING THE WORK WEEK

Another example of our principles shows what can happen when personal incentives are a way of life. Baptist Hospital began operation in the days when the forty-eight-hour week for service departments was standard for the area. It was not long before shorter schedules were an objective. To reduce the work week nearly 10 percent, the obvious course is to add enough people to make up the difference. However, we approached the objective with a different strategy.

Several months before our target date, we told department heads they could go to a forty-four-hour week as soon as each could reach target performance without added staff. On the average, the departments succeeded in meeting that objective in less than a month. Those who ask "Why hasn't this been tried before?" must recognize that the hours situation was similar to many other ideas: "We have always done it this way, so this way must be the right way." Frequently, that's nonsense.

Later, we used the sample principle to move down to a forty-hour work week. In both instances hospital management refrained from telling staff *how* to do it. Instead, people were challenged to find ways to work more effectively. Our supervisors discovered activities that really were not needed; and by eliminating these and scheduling more carefully, they found that it *was* possible to carve 10 percent or more out of the work week and still provide top quality. Everyone profited.

However, as was pointed out at the time, this sort of action is possible with universal benefit only when productivity per person goes *up!* People need an incentive to want to do better; in this case, it was having an extra half day off every week. Once the productivity plan was in effect, it was more money in the paycheck. But, as our country has learned in recent years, increasing payments *without* commensurate productivity means inflation. It's a hard lesson.

PROOF THAT INCENTIVES WORK

That lesson was illustrated in several other ways in the early 1960s, ways which gave added emphasis to the productivity experiments.

The first was the acceptance of statistical results published regularly by Hospital Administrative Services (HAS). The HAS figures gave hospitals a benchmark against which to judge their performance. From the first, those statistics helped reinforce what our management strongly believed: generally speaking, the hospital's best departments statistically were also the best in terms of service. By 1964 there was growing interest in this subject and I was asked to provide a study for *Hospitals* magazine* which underscored this point. Quoting a study made in four localities, I reported that there was substantial evidence that hospitals preferred by patients were those which paid personnel the

---

* Pat N. Groner, "Hospital Administrative Services: How Hospitals Gain by HAS Comparison," *Hospitals, JAHA,* May 16, 1964, pp. 54–58.

highest salaries, yet had the lowest charges. It was, as pointed out, an example of free enterprise at work; high productivity and administrative controls made the two seemingly incompatible factors work for everyone's benefit.

In 1951, when Baptist Hospital opened, rates and charges were quite low, certainly below state and national averages; the local wage scale paralleled charges. For over a decade, with economies of size and experience, Baptist continued to maintain its relative position of low charges but succeeded in boosting salaries until they approached the state average (though they remained 15 to 18 percent below the national mean). The appendix statistical tables in Appendix C on those comparisons tell this story.

Then came the great day when the administrative team could see the end in sight for the expansion of 1963–64. This was a substantial effort; it involved only thirty beds, a 10 percent increase, but added were thousands of square feet of working area, new larger work areas for some disciplines, and the introduction of several others. For a modest institution it was a major undertaking and in an average setting such growth automatically means additional staffing.

Holding the Line on the Laundry Bill

Baptist's people reacted no differently. As opening day approached, each department head sharpened his pencil and presented his request. In those cases where activities were related to patient volume, the asking was a staffing increase of 10 percent; in a few situations related to the hospital's total area (such as Housekeeping), it was even higher.

The assistant administrator that year was a young man, John Schill. John was responsible for nonprofessional services and, as a student of management, had a keen insight into this kind of detail. Looking at the Laundry, for instance, he developed some interesting deductions.

Up to that point, the Laundry, whose equipment and location were only five years old, was staffed largely by men and women graduates of commercial establishments. It was running about 30 percent better than comparable hospitals, judging from HAS statistics. However, there were some interesting sidelights. Each month Baptist's Laundry was charging some eighty hours of overtime to do its work. Linen production varied by days, with high totals on Mondays (to catch up for weekend days when the department was idle) and lesser volumes the other days until a fairly low point was reached on Fridays. There was a fair share of machine downtime, and supply utilization and linen damage were tangible, though still below average.

Probing these details, Schill began asking himself this question:

What would happen in our *new* situation if we got these people to really work smarter? Could we avoid hiring more people if we had an incentive to make the present operators more conscientious?

Schill met with the department's supervisor, Arthur Bellamy, and laid these questions before him. Bellamy was hesitant; after all, *incentive* was a new word in his business. And since the people involved were unsophisticated, explaining such a system might be hard.

John persevered. "Suppose," he pressed, "suppose that by doing this we could add up to 15 percent to their paychecks? Think they'd be able to understand *that?*

"Everyone wants a raise," the department head responded. "Why not talk about it to the people, see what they say?"

Schill went back to his data charts and ultimately devised a formula he felt would work IF the climate was right. Together, we went over each detail.

At this point an employee meeting was arranged to outline the situation in elementary terms.

1. The Laundry had been producing quality results.
2. Based on comparisons with other hospitals, the volume of work was above average.
3. There was often a lot of overtime because of machine downtime.
4. The amount of supplies used (bleach, detergent, allied chemicals) was inconsistent; in some months about what it should be, in other periods unrealistically high.
5. The hospital was about to add thirty additional beds, meaning some 10 percent more pounds of linen per week.
6. That work could be done within a regular shift if the machine downtime could be eliminated. Substantial sums could also be saved by using supplies more carefully.

Then he made his proposal: "I'll tell you what we'd like to try, *if* you're willing. I'd like to see if we can take care of this extra volume of linen with our SAME crew. If we could do that, here's what Baptist is willing to try. In getting ready for this expansion, Mr. Bellamy figured the department should add one more person. We'll take the money he would have been paid and put it in a pot along with supply savings, and divide *half* with you. That is, we'll give each of you a share of it every month . . . if you can produce the linen with acceptable quality. We'll use this last six months as a measuring time on supply use, too, and we'll share any savings you can produce. If the saving is $10, we'll put $5 in the pot to be shared, and the patients will get the other $5 . . . through lower charges."

Actually, the full formula included the following:

1. Linen produced above 115,000 pounds per month would carry a productivity value of 2.5 cents per pound.
2. Deductions from the total would be for:
   a. Supply costs above the maximum range for the following items and rates:

Detergent Type I	@ 0.140 per pound—550–600 lbs.
Bleach	0.045 per pound—400–450 lbs.
Softener	0.359 per pound—300–500 lbs.
Detergent Type II	0.118 per pound—700–800 lbs.

   b. Overtime at $1.00 per hour.

All employees were to share equally, and shares would be determined by computing total value of the production share, subtracting items for overtime and supplies (when applicable), and dividing the balance among the number of people. Schill repeated that any dollars that had to be paid out as overtime would be deducted from the amount available for sharing.

There were lots of questions. People wanted to know how much they might receive as extra earnings; and they wanted to know what would happen if the plan did not work, or if they did not feel they could do the work at the faster pace. Schill put his answers in straightforward terms.

The way I figure it, if we can eliminate overtime and work at a normal pace, keeping the machines maintained and running as they should, you'll have no trouble getting the job done.

Second, we both recognize that this is an experiment. I'm experimenting; so are you. We'll set up a reasonable trial period, and at the end of that time if the plan isn't fair we'll end it. However, I want everyone to remember that this *is* a trial, and changes might be needed in the formula. The savings to the hospital will be changes that will help us control the cost of care to our patients, so we have to be totally fair. I want that understood, okay?"

The test began. The results proved that John Schill was a very good man with a slide rule (and an astute judge of human character). Those basic entry level people quickly displayed that they had some industrial engineering talents of their own! New handling techniques crept into their procedures, which proved superior to those in the laundry association's manual. A new sense of teamwork emerged.

Machine malfunctions diminished, and supply usage settled into a flat curve ... on target, week after week. Linen production for the enlarged hospital was achieved with virtually no overtime. Employees who then were earning about $225 per month began receiving incentive checks of from $35 to $40 per month (1965 dollars). Equally significant, the people found a new joy in achievement; they were proud of their accomplishments, had a new sense of well being, and in short order spread their story to friends in other departments.

Monthly Meetings That Are Worth the Time

Another plus realized early in the process was the byplay in the monthly review meetings that Schill established as part of the system.

Administration had always recommended monthly supervisor–employee meetings as a means of generating communication. But frequently in the past management people avoided them because they sometimes degenerated into complaint sessions, or there was seemingly nothing to say beyond pointing up problems or shortcomings. Now things were different. Schill recalls the sequence this way: "We decided that the employee meeting would be the appropriate time to distribute the incentive checks. We purposely put these earnings into separate checks (we even printed the checks differently); this made certain there would be no misunderstanding of what the checks were, and also tended to keep families from counting the incentive as part of the regular pay. Incentive earnings *could* be affected by unforeseen events, and we wanted that to remain clear. As part of the discussion the supervisor went over the month's results, step by step, showing where the savings came from and covering special incidents that affected those results. This gave employees an opportunity to offer their point of view, to help in planning the next month's work, and to work around difficult situations that might adversely affect their earnings."

THE DATA BASE LESSON

Of course, there were problems. Most stemmed from a data base that was inadequate, since earlier production figures were not complete. As Arthur Bellamy expressed it: "Once the incentive went in, we were weighing the laundry bags and mops; before, we didn't care to handle them twice so we just washed them."

That need caused John and me to look carefully at all future formulas. For, without solid historical data, it's impossible to develop a valid program. Recently, that need caused the hospital to take a new and more professional turn, as the reader will discover.

The attitude of the people can probably best be summed up in a statement made several years later by one of the women as she was about to retire. She told me: "Mr. Groner, I just want you to know how much I think of this hospital for starting the incentive plan. I have worked all of my life, and that was the *first* time anyone had given me a chance to have a say in the way I worked and what I took home. I thought that was mighty good."

Incentive checks became a way of life in the Laundry, and employees in other departments began asking "How can we get in on this?"

That was just what John Schill and I were hoping for.

Chapter 2

Hospitals and the Rest of the Economy

LOOKING BACK

Historians argue about when and where the first formal hospital was created. If you vote for Rome under Constantine or thirteenth century Paris, I would not dispute you. Either date verifies that houses of healing go back a long time. Yet no matter what country or century you choose, including our own country's first effort, Pennsylvania Hospital of 1751, the establishments were charitable in character, based on philanthropic good will offerings and religious compassion. Benjamin Franklin, one of the incorporators of the Philadelphia institution, sparked the project by going among friends to raise money. Ten generations later his descendents on that board of trustees are still doing the same!

Beginning in the last decade of the eighteenth century, religious orders in America launched their superb role in building hospitals. From New York to Salt Lake City, from the Southern Baptist Southland to the cloisters of Emmitsburg, Maryland, men and women followed the call of the Judeo–Christian ethic (or nonprofit voluntary care motive) and gave of their talents and their purses to provide hospitals. Americans developed simple, labor-intensive institutions whose budgets were the concern of the wealthy or the religious order or denomination and whose spirit was love and charity.

It is hard to believe that just twenty-five years ago those values were still the driving force behind hospital care in America! Speaking from experience, I can recall the management philosophies that pervaded most hospitals. The addition of a new piece of equipment (or even a whole new wing) was often a matter of personal philanthropy; and, as

11

little as twenty years ago, hospitals of 200 and more beds budgeted only a few thousand dollars annually for equipment improvements!

Salaries limped along at basic levels, too, kept low by an enduring belief that nurses were "dedicated" and thus need not be paid on a scale paralleling other professions. There was only a handful of paramedical personnel in those days, for the wave of technology had not yet come. Even though growing numbers of Americans were insured through Blue Cross and commercial health plans, as a nation we were still far from health oriented. Some people still went to a hospital only under duress.

But the past twenty years have seen hospitals become the hub of health care and treatment; the technical revolution, spurred in part by space age developments and the computer, has flooded the land. Where once the hospital was labor-intensive, now it is capital intensive, too. Baptist Hospital, which spent just $8,000 for new equipment in 1954, spent over $1 million in twelve months only twenty years later (and that hardly realized the hopes of the medical staff, whose members had more wants than the budget could supply.)

The advent of technology heralded a new paramedical society also. And, as health care became more exciting, it plunged into the family television room in living color, popularizing the medical miracles of this generation. People lost their fears of hospitals, education promoted more and better health scrutiny, more elective and diagnostic procedures. When the federal government made Medicare and Medicaid the law of the land, patient totals swelled steadily.

Although results for hospitals themselves might have been predictable, few managers have had time to prepare for the rush of change.

Demands for skilled people created scarcity, and scarcity promoted price and salary competition. Larger numbers of employees, some of them semiskilled, attracted unions; unions negotiated higher benefits. Where unions were not a factor, comparative opportunities acted as the bargaining force.

The process became a repetitive cycle. The health care progress generated patronage, higher utilization stimulated growth, growth fostered larger establishments, which in turn gradually ended the closeknit personal relationships that had characterized employment in hospitals for centuries.

Large size is often not a blessing; most hospitals have found it a mixed bag at best. For with economies of scale came the threat of inefficiency, of opportunities for loss, theft, waste, malingering, payroll padding, empire building, and the other ills that develop when communication lines become extended. Some hospitals lost their intimate concern for the care of the patient and the well being of the institution.

I cannot speak for all hospitals, of course, and I would be unfair if I sounded a blanket indictment. But I suspect there are few among the nation's larger institutions that have not suffered many of these problems. These ills came to be because hospitals grew rapidly with little chance to build into their operations the cost consciousness and accountability that make private industry and commerce successful.

Instead, hospitals continued to be managed by the same rules as before. Indices of efficiency were primarily measurements against fellow hospitals; institutions often operated under dissimilar conditions and circumstances. Even into the 1960s, deficit financing of operations was a common practice, with administration and board willing to "pass the hat" at year's end among the benefactors. Industrial engineering, that unique semiscience that has meant much to the production of mass produced goods, was only occasionally mentioned in hospitals. When it became obvious to a hospital management that costs were outstripping charges, the answer was to raise charges! Even that archaic measuring device—the cost per patient day—remained inviolate as the national measuring standard, despite the fact that in America the rest of the economy is based on *prices*. (Example: Consumer *Price* Index but *cost* per patient per day.)

A decade ago, two additional factors entered the picture, government reimbursement of care (with government imposed controls) and the consumerism movement. Both introduced players in the game who are powerful, vocal, unpredictable and, to a degree, ill informed about the general mechanics of health care. With their coming, pressures on hospitals mounted to an explosive level.

It is no secret that federal economists either misinterpreted (or chose not to believe) the pre-1966 estimates of what government-sponsored health care would cost. Either way, federal fiscal policies suffered a mild coronary almost immediately, and today are far from restored. As a result, what came was a frantic policing of hospital methods, establishing on the way reimbursement practices that cut heavily into the average institution's well-being. Even at the beginning, when Medicare was mailing its first checks, a few in the Department of Health, Education, and Welfare saw signs that made them ask:

- "Why is there no pressure in hospitals for efficiency?"
- "Where are the industrial engineers?"
- "How come there are no incentive plans there?"
- And succinctly: "Why are costs and charges so different among seemingly comparable institutions?"

A few asked that strategic question, but they took no strong action. Others passed legislation and implemented regulations forcing hospitals to perpetuate the contrived economic environment in which they were being forced to operate. Instead, even when the nation was placed under a system of price controls, federal bureaucrats adopted a sort of "anti-incentive," basing allowances on prior *cost* figures, never getting down to brass tacks to question obviously higher figures. Thus, the hospital that historically had worked hard to be efficient and to keep its costs and charges low, was penalized, while its inefficient neighbor was paid a bonus for poor management.

Now however, there are signs of change. Legislation and rulings are coming on the scene that give emphasis to the hospital doing its managerial homework. Still, these moves are not an all-out effort to create an economic environment based on free enterprise, which is what the nation needs to achieve results.

THE INDUSTRIAL EXAMPLE

Americans sometimes mistakenly believe that their early countrymen were blessed with a sort of second sight that enabled them to harness efficiency to the inventive genius inherent in our industrial revolution. That isn't so. Eli Whitney deserves credit for the concept of manufacturing with interchangeable parts, and a host of tinkerers and mechanical wizards are lauded for turning our young country toward countless mechanical innovations which made "things" possible. Prior to 1900, inexpensive goods usually resulted from operating mines and mills with distressingly low wage scales. The organizational concept and our modern motivational system were still half a century away. Hospitals of the nineteenth century paralleled their industrial cousins in all of this.

I suspect that, when the small family farm became too inefficient to compete and its owners fled to the city to find work, America might well have been on its way to socialism had the genius of a few brilliant people not made it possible for the workingman to earn a greater share for what he did. In 1900, the principal differences between a knitting mill in the Carolinas and a hospital were the working conditions and the modest prestige that came from helping the sick. Pay scales were much the same. In the next thirty years, several key steps helped escalate industrial wages; but, by and large, hospital pay remained static.

Much of the credit for industrial wage growth belongs to a handful of trained "industrial engineers;" Frederick Taylor and Frank and Lillian Gilbreth are the best remembered (the pair also is recalled as the father and mother in *Cheaper By The Dozen*). Taylor and the Gilbreths recognized that there was a certain magic in organizing and simplifying work, in developing work situations where fatigue was minimized, in streamlining work flow to eliminate unnecessary transportation of materials, lifting, pushing, or product storage. During World War I the fruits of their work made it possible for war industries to create incredible quantities of materials, using productivity methods theretofore largely untried in most businesses.

Two examples that illustrate the changes involved Alvah Roebuck and Alfred Sloan. Roebuck, looking ahead, recognized before the turn of the century the need to merchandise at the point of the consumer. By establishing dependable merchandising policies, he succeeded in turning a small mail order business into the nation's largest retail outlet, reaching out to millions of Americans who lived on farms, away from easy access to products they needed. By introducing manufacturing and purchasing efficiencies and a warehousing/distribution system that was new, Roebuck made his company an international consumer purchase byword. Later, when the automobile was on its way to changing the life style and mobility of the farm family, this same company was sufficiently farsighted to make well-stocked retail and catalog order outlets easily accessible to everyone. As catalog buying diminished, Sears shopping centers were born. It was a unique way of merchandising—of using the skills of people—of meeting a need.

A similar story relates to Alfred Sloan. In the early 1920s the Ford Motor Company was gradually grinding scores of smaller competitors into the ground. Sloan, seeing the need for economies of scale and wise use of facilities, grouped together five separate motor car companies, each with its sales target on a different plateau of the American breadbasket. The formation of General Motors provided a huge, stable company which restored competition—and which made the wisest use of materials, productivity methods, and merchandise. These are only two of the great success stories of this period. There were others in oil, steel, transportation, mining, and milling. But this management-centered revolution had little application to hospitals at the time.

The industrial and commercial managers and their followers introduced still another element to their efficiency equation: the motivational incentive.

Actually, these students of productivity were not utilizing a new idea in America. The earliest English settlements established precedent. At Jamestown settlers first devised a sort of communal existence, each family assigned to community work, each living from common stores. The result: they almost starved to death! Captain John Smith gets much of the credit for turning this situation around. His method was to allot each family personal tracts of land on which to grow their food, except for a modest share to be allotted to common stores, a form of taxes. Not surprisingly, the situation in Virginia quickly improved. It was work or starve, and people responded as they have through all of human history.

Other similar illustrations dot the pages of American lore, from New Harmony to the Grange, from cooperatives to early experiments in common ownership of banks. The message was clear: WHERE THE WORKMAN HELPS DETERMINE HIS METHOD, AND WHERE HE WILL SHARE IN THE RESULTS IN PROPORTION TO HIS OUTPUT, PRODUCTION AND EFFICIENCY SOAR. When a man is paid a common wage without incentive, his interest and productivity frequently flag.

Thus engineers of the twentieth century attacked the problem of how to improve the interest *and* the output of the production worker. The first answer was obvious: pay people in proportion to what they did. Establish a basic level of output that must be met to remain on the job, then give the worker a portion of the gains derived from production above that level. Engineers gave this concept many names—incentive bonus, piecework rates, group incentives, and production rewards, to list a few. In most instances, the plans enjoyed a degree of success; companies enjoyed added output, workers profited, purchasers were able to buy goods less expensively. From the Model T to breakfast food, Americans enjoyed a spectrum of mass produced goods, and the workers who manned the shop lines were better able to enjoy the fruits of their labors.

However, incentives were not all peaches and cream. Countless companies visualized incentives as a purely statistical tool, attempting to squeeze production people instead of encouraging them. In short, they introduced only half a loaf; these companies had recognized the effectiveness of exhorting effort but had omitted the motivational potential present in incentives. Sadly, it took portions of industry a quarter century to recognize this failing and to remedy the problem. Some, unfortunately, have not learned the lessons yet; their relations with employees, and often their status among consumers, illustrates this.

Please note that I am *not* suggesting that there is but one way to develop a productivity program. The potential mechanics are legion. From Baptist Hospital's experience, I learned that there *are* some essentials needed if a program is to succeed and be long lived.

1. A company or institution must believe that there is a need for the incentive and must do its homework in defining objectives.
2. Management must *really* believe that employee welfare is impor-

tant and that it is management's responsibility to see that employee earnings are as high as possible, commensurate with the financial health of the institution.

3. There must be a true correlation between an incentive program and the welfare of the customer—or patient.

4. The organization must recognize that incentives are not static, but require continual updating and policing to keep them relevant.

5. The organization must be prepared to make employees "partners" in business, to take them into the management's confidence, to want and use employee counsel.

6. There must be recognition of the fact that no two organizations are the same and that a program tailormade for one may require considerable restructuring to work in another.

HOSPITALS DISCOVER PRODUCTIVITY

All of this—the background, the philosophy, the use of incentives in industry and the success of the American system—is common textbook knowledge, but not as applied to the hospital. In the years since the Second World War volumes have been written on the subject, and many countries, such as Japan and West Germany, have adopted these methods too. Involving people has been commonplace strategy, though the methods have varied. Participation, motivation, and financial incentives helped remove some abrasive elements which once threatened industrial peace. In short, the incentive concept is a success in business.

But as all of this was taking form and proving its worth in business, hospital productivity and incentive systems remained taboo! Part of the reason was the belief that incentives and production line techniques were inseparable; that introduction of "efficiency methods" was an invitation to less compassionate care. "We're dealing with human life, not machines or nuts and bolts," was a fairly representative answer.

Another factor, I suspect, was the continuing belief that the attendance by large numbers of warm bodies was equivalent to offering good health care. Nearly thirty years of personal experience has revealed instances where hospitals were staffed with larger than necessary numbers of low paid, scantily trained people who tried to make up in sheer numbers what they lacked in ability. What seemed like TLC (tender loving care) was really ineffective and inefficient care. But the patients did not know this, and so for a long time such remained the *modus operandi* in many institutions.

Then, as inflation and allied pressures of the 1960s became apparent, a new factor entered the picture. Citizens and writers began to make outraged statements about rising health care costs. From *Redbook* to the *Reader's Digest,* authors attacked hospitals, and the daily news media had many unkind things to say about hospital charges.

Of course, the escalation in costs and charges was not unexpected. Much of the technical advance in care in that decade had a high cost orientation. The pressures for skills, the cost of expansion, and new problems such as greater demand for parking space, pushed hospitals further into a fiscal corner. Unlike manufacturing counterparts, hospitals could not rely upon methods engineering and incentives to help pare the burden. Instead, hospital managers responded with a time-honored fiscal means; they raised rates and charges, time after time.

Later, as critics attacked other targets and began to protest the refinements of care, some institutions stepped up their dependence on another long-time remedy: more people, coupled with infusions of often wasteful, counterproductive government regulation.

More people, more expensive people, larger establishments, more technology, more safeguards, higher insurance premiums, more sophisticated supplies ... these and many more elements swarmed in on the chief executive and his board. As mentioned earlier, federal regulations, including rate regulation, worked to the advantage of the inefficient operator. Charges, frozen at high prior levels, gave no credit to institutions operating with a strong concern for costs.

I suppose the best summary I know of this situation came about three years ago when our hospital entertained several foreign health experts. As part of their orientation, I tried to explain these problems and was interrupted by one of the men who said: "If there is one place on earth where efficiency can be integrated into a health delivery system, it should be in the United States. Why is it you've remained so fragmented?"

That was a difficult question to answer.

Chapter 3

Selling the Product

Anyone who sells a product will tell you that word of mouth praise is the most effective advertising and that if you can get people to come seeking your product in time of scarcity, *then* you've got the psychology on your side!

That was almost the way things were for us at Baptist Hospital once the Laundry staff began to enjoy those monthly productivity incentive checks. People from other departments began asking questions: "When are we going to get some of that productivity?", they demanded.

Hospital management was as anxious as they were, I suspect, although there were some obvious roadblocks. The concept in the laundry had jelled because Baptist was entering a new demand situation. There was an obvious opportunity, for there was a tailormade lump sum of wage funds to work from. Finding formulas in other situations would not be that easy.

There was another big factor, too. John Schill was a capable manager, but not an industrial engineer. Our hospital did not have one, and there were none in the area specializing in hospitals. Whatever was done was going to have to be done on an experimental basis. At this point Baptist did involve its management-personnel consultant as an assistant, for communications were becoming increasingly important as we proceeded.

COMMUNICATING THE PLAN

Reviewing those early years, perhaps the greatest failing was that not enough time was spent planning communications. Most critical, some supervisors failed to do a thorough job of communicating regularly. That was and *is* critical. One value in this plan rests on the regular

19

review of what happened and the *why* behind incentive earnings. If an employee group had a good incentive month, people needed to know why. If the reverse was true, it was equally important to reconstruct the reasons. Most of Baptist's management people recognized this and did a fine job. A few did not, and invariably their plans got into trouble. Naturally, administration must bear the stigma of not having prepared those department heads thoroughly. It is a point that cannot be overemphasized.

Also, John Schill and I felt we needed a broader brainstorming base to identify fundamentals for incorporation in formulas and elements of timing. It did not take long to realize that there were only a few similarities that could be counted upon from department to department, and that in some situations there probably would be some actual opposition based on feelings of professionalism or hangups induced by past philosophies.

John and I did not hurry. With this experiment working well, we were determined to proceed first in areas where there was a high chance of success, or where opportunities for savings to hospital and patient seemed highest. We agreed as a team to postpone action in departments where it was not possible to justify what was to be tried. Thus, it was important to ultimate success to proceed slowly, with homework done well. There was never any thought of trying to install programs everywhere simultaneously, or of waiting to introduce other new sections until a large number of departments could be serviced at once. That caused discontent among a few employees who were anxious to participate; but it certainly prevented headaches—and probably a lot of mistakes.

What was learned in the formula research?

First, the relationship with Laundry personnel confirmed the value of the training directors' old slogan, K.I.S.S. ("Keep it simple, stupid"). Industrial firms had often 'turned off' employees by using formulas people could not understand. John Schill wanted to make the incentive plan both a financial tool *and* a motivator for good work and quality; to achieve this people had to be able to see and discuss the methods.

Second, historic data searches disclosed that there were several easy to survey factors that had a more or less common usage. Most departments had a "pounds of linen processed," "meals served," "numbers of examinations completed," "operations performed," or similar mathematical measurement that could be examined to determine a base. All departments had manpower, hours worked, overtime, or similar considerations. And almost all departments were involved with supply utilization, utilities economy, or similar items which had a correlation to work performed and the cost of operating the department.

With this kind of thinking resolved, Baptist's team developed an order for formula determination that went something like this:

1. Gather historical data on the operation.
2. Review the short term economic history of the department.
3. Compare departmental results with national averages.
4. Select meaningful criteria that can be understood by all participants.
5. Use simple mathematics to produce a formula that will include factors over which the employees have reasonable control.
6. Apply all of these to counter existing shortcomings and overcome problems.
7. Project current operating data against the formula.
8. Attempt to set a date for introducing the formula when some event, either manpower attrition, enlargement of volume, or the like might provide a challenge for a lesser group to accomplish more, as had been the case in the laundry.

Once a workable mechanism was determined for a department, discussions were held with key supervisors and department heads to get their reactions and to invite criticism. Then, the program would be presented to employees, using group meetings.

THE RADIOLOGY EXPERIENCE

One of the earliest attempts was in Radiology. This was a department with excellent results, yet some obvious opportunities existed for saving salary dollars. Historically, this department had heavy technical activity during morning hours and a lessened load after about one o'clock. The clerical staff had an opposite routine. A first judgment was that this staff, with three secretaries in a group of twelve (including technicians and orderlies) was probably too large. After looking at the work patterns, it seemed logical to get the technical staff to help with some of the materials organization for the secretaries during the lower activity afternoon period, and to rearrange clerical requirements to permit help to the technicians in the morning.

In the midst of these discussions at the administrative level, the senior secretary announced her retirement. That provided an opening!

The formula developed was based on maintaining a high procedures load with reduced manhours; it recognized quantity of procedures; it also included an opportunity for supply control. At the time there were eleven staff members involved, and the formula presented to them looked like this:

Standard Cost Per Procedure　=　$4.70

Actual Cost Per Procedure　=　$\dfrac{\text{Salary + Supply Expense (YTD)}}{\text{Procedures (YTD)}}$

Total Share Value　=　Actual Cost Per Procedure x Total Procedures

Results were consistent with previous experience. Despite a drop in procedures, the x-ray department increased productivity, reduced its cost per procedure, and, in general, improved performance. On the average, month after month, radiology people drew incentive checks averaging over $30, and the quality of work, as measured by the radiologists' evaluations and patient opinion polls, improved.

THE OPERATING SUITE

The operating suite was one area where I had serious doubts that an incentive plan could bear fruit. The OR's performance, measured against HAS standards, was just too good. Yet, because the people were so productive, management looked for a method of recognizing what was already being done and perhaps improving further by isolating some cost factors.

The initial OR incentive plan was to reward the group for outstanding results rather than concentrate on labor savings. To do this, the first formula concentrated on departmental gross earnings, with individual incentive shares adjusted on the percentage relationship between supply expense to gross earnings and gross profit to gross earnings. Using historic data as a base, established monthly levels were set that could be adjusted up or down depending on experience.

This encouraged proper charging for work performed and supply control. Reduced use of supplies would thus affect the share value, and added departmental income would, too, although this was not anticipated because our scheduling was already so thorough. Again, this was a singularly productive department, and the formula base recognized this.

Results surprised everyone. Mrs. Zelda Bowman, the supervisor of long standing, did a remarkable job of communicating the goals and of encouraging her people to examine their procedures. They questioned procedures critically where supply costs seemed abnormal.

Asking "Why do we do it this way?", staff found numerous places where supplies could be trimmed. One case involved sutures. Physician preference had created a practice of vials of suture to be broken beyond need. Revising this had a substantial effect.

New, more careful checks on instruments reduced losses. There were others, too, so many that in the first full year of the plan, the OR record looked like this:

	1964	1965
Operations	7,969	8,055
Supplies	$ 91,734.00	$ 85,522.00
Supply cost per operation	11.51	10.61
Earnings	$309,572.00	$337,847.00

That was the way our OR formula began. Before long it was apparent that we had underestimated the true potential within that group, and the formula was redrafted to include a genuine productivity element. During this period OR employees shared a total incentive of $3,529 for the remainder of 1965, and $8,132 the following year—with activity up and supply costs down.

MORE BASIC INCENTIVE PLANS

In an entirely different kind of operation, a more basic plan was installed in the coffee shop. Historically, our coffee shop had been a sort of plus and minus operation; turnover had been above average. There were the usual public relations problems from time to time, and there were suspicions of supply theft, unreported charges when favorites were served, and some pure carelessness.

The 1965 incentive plan placed operations under the charge of a lead waitress on each shift. Emphasis was placed on both productivity *and* profits. Lead waitresses were paid 5 percent of gross profits in excess of $1,500 per month; other employees received 3 percent. Since profits depend on customer volume and satisfaction (as well as proper charges), the abuses faded, attitudes improved, and employees found incentive earnings creeping up. Later, as will be discussed, this philosophy of incentives in a nonprofit institution came under challenge from the Internal Revenue Service, which claimed that the incentive or "profits" endanger the tax-exempt status of the hospital, even in so small a unit where operations are seemingly unrelated to the major emphasis of the institution.

Another simpler situation involved the EEG unit. This was a one-woman operation which had been recently transferred to the hospital from a psychiatrist's office. The technician had worked for the doctor for some years, and her routine was well established. Even though there frequently were greater numbers of service requests, she *would not* or *could not* deviate from her habit pattern of two cases in the morning, one in the afternoon. There were no great supply savings potentials; instead, this appeared to be an incentive situation of classical piecework orientation.

The approach made to the technician was classical, too. The hospital suggested that it might be able to control charges to patients if volume could be increased and proposed that a dollar incentive would be given to her and to the hospital on patients served above her present level. At that time, the EEG charge was $25.00; the formula said that for every procedure made above three in the workday, the technician would earn an added $2.50, and the hospital would receive $2.50. Projecting this still further, the proposal said that EEG charges could be reduced if volume reached 70 each month.

The technician was the typical "Ms. Reluctant;" she maintained stoutly that her historic pattern assured quality and was the maximum that could be done with precision and safety. Yet within a month, the department's output was up five procedures, and the second month the total climbed from 63 to 82! Because she was a one-woman department, she held no departmental meetings to explain the results—John Schill and I often wondered what she said to herself.

And so the incentive program moved ahead.

One by one, other departments installed plans. Some, like Medical Records, Housekeeping, and Coffee Shop moved into gear easily. Others were more difficult to formalize because the factors were ill-defined. Nursing in particular provided a challenge, where formulas had to be revised repeatedly as methods and circumstances changed.

It's important at this point to recognize this fact; it required over two years to develop programs for the several departments. By then, approximately 80 percent of hospital employees were participating in some form of incentive, and results were beginning to attract nationwide attention. All this did not happen overnight; there were many pitfalls and some temporary failures. But the concept progressed steadily, and the hospital industry was becoming interested.

NURSING: THE LARGEST CHALLENGE

The greatest challenge came in providing a suitable formula for nursing personnel. This, after all, was our largest employee unit; they handled the greatest volume of supplies, were involved in the greatest fluctuation in activity, and, consequently, had a huge opportunity to improve use of manhours.

There were also some perplexing questions related to the nursing formula. When one begins to consider the overall hospital operation, it becomes apparent that nursing interfaces intimately with others. The efficiency of drug administration and Pharmacy is certainly linked to nursing procedures. Purchasing, warehousing, and central supply methods are largely devised to mesh with activities on the nursing floors. Even linen from the laundry is tied in both demand and inventories to procedures devised by the nursing staff.

When we tried to isolate nursing from these activities, we found that we were about to promote injustices that could sabotage our efforts. We were seeking new avenues of cooperation, and that proved to be one of our first overall benefits! This investigation forced our management team to study these relationships, and what we discovered unearthed some costly practices. The examination also opened our eyes to some petty rivalries that had arisen between the various disciplines—differences which, once overcome, enhanced the hospital's ability to serve well. I'll cite just one example.

We were concerned by the statistics on linen. Sheets and pillow cases seemed to evaporate. No matter how the subject was addressed, the losses continued. Laundry pleaded innocence; nursing supervision claimed that they had trouble getting enough to maintain operations. Management suspected much of the linen was going out the door. Thus, when we built our first nursing formula, we put heavy emphasis on supply usage, including linens. Other supplies were included, too, and soon enjoyed similar savings. But linen was a prize example.

With the formula in use, the true story began to surface. Over the years, many nurses *believed* that linen was in short supply; consequently, they would overrequisition. However, once checks began they could not overinventory at the nursing station. So nurses quietly started placing the excess they felt they needed in the bureaus in patient rooms. From that rather obvious location, countless sheets, towels, and pillow cases simply disappeared! Who took them? I could not say. But month after month *until* the nurses themselves began to profit from savings in linen utilization, losses continued. Once the nurses' saving became a dollar and cents factor to them, they stopped hoarding and accepted the delivery routine, which had always been adequate. The net result was a continuing savings to the hospital, adequate linen supplies, and income to the nurses.

There were other problems in setting a nursing pattern; one was scheduling. A hospital's manpower allocations are somewhat different from most other businesses. We can anticipate many census highs and lows, yet many times supervisors have been slow to alter staffing to meet these fluctuations—largely because to do so takes effort and often produces some degree of unhappiness. Hospital people enjoy holidays and vacations; wise scheduling enables accommodation with actual institutional demands. Careful study of historical data and application of appropriate manhours per patient day can make an enormous difference in the cost of one year's care. But some natural resistance to altered scheduling surfaced, until the employees began to share in the dollars such enlightened scheduling produced. Table 3–1 demonstrates the improvement in staffing patterns resulting from the stimulation of productivity incentive. Both understaffing and total manhours were reduced simply by more sensible control of excess manhours. For instance, prior to the plan in nursing, we had suffered for years with a shortage of fulltime registered nurses. The difference had to be made up by recruiting numerous part-time people. But then someone had a thought: Why not make incentive earnings applicable for fulltime people only? There were a few risks involved, but we decided to go ahead. Immediately, five parttime RNs found that they could work full time—and, although this didn't completely overcome this shortage, it certainly helped.

The major criticism of such a philosophy lies in the belief by some that concentration on minimized manhours will lead to diminished care quality. That subject is addressed in subsequent chapters. At this point, the significant comment would be: virtually everything we have studied or experienced refutes that argument. Quality is seldom a result of high numbers. It results from organization, education, and motivation. We believe that our results have confirmed this.

FOUR OTHER EXAMPLES

Our efforts in Laboratory began in 1966. The recently completed expansion was producing expected growth, and both our pathologists and the chief technologist had petitioned for a staffing increase. Following the techniques used in other departments, an incentive plan succeeded in rearranging schedules and duty hours. Initial response from staff was good, and the staffing increase request was withdrawn.

But then we encountered one of the serious drawbacks of our total program—a failing which resulted from a classic communications breakdown. The department's normal operations were excellent because we had a topnotch chief technologist who communicated extremely well and possessed a strong personal relationship with her staff. But when it came to the incentive plan, her communications proved lacking. A key

Table 3-1 Nursing Department Staffing Comparisons June 1966 to June 1967

Service		Direct Nursing Hours Per Patient Day				Sat-Sun Staffing			Hi-Low	Excess Hours	Days of Staffing		
		Goal (Departmental goals of hours necessary for ideal staffing)	High (Highest day of hours per patient during the month)	Low (Lowest day of hours per patient during the month)	Aver. (Average hours per patient day for the month)	Aver. (Average hours per patient day for weekends)	Above Wk.Day (Excess of weekend staffing over weekday)	Above Goal (Hours per patient day above desired goal on weekend coverage)	Spread (Difference between high and low staffing days during month)	Over Goal (Excess of average staffing above goal)	Over Goal	Under Goal	On Goal
Orthopedics	1966	3.5	5.8	3.3	4.3	4.55	.25	1.05	2.5	.80	27	2	1
	1967		4.1	3.1	3.35	3.60	.25	.10	1.0	-.15	5	11	14
Surgical	1966	3.5	4.8	3.3	3.8	4.33	.53	.83	1.5	.30	24	2	4
	1967		4.1	3.0	3.56	3.73	.17	.23	1.1	.06	13	5	12
Gynecology	1966	3.5	4.6	3.0	3.7	3.98	.28	.48	1.6	.20	20	6	4
	1967		4.1	3.1	3.53	3.75	.22	.25	1.0	.03	9	5	16
Obstetrics	1966	3.5	6.2	3.3	4.1	4.38	.28	.88	2.9	.60	23	1	6
	1967		5.9	2.8	3.62	3.95	.33	.45	3.1	.12	11	12	7
Medicine	1966	3.5	5.0	3.3	4.0	4.57	.57	1.07	1.7	.50	24	3	3
	1967		3.9	3.1	3.6	3.63	.03	.13	.8	.10	6	9	15
Psychiatry	1966	5.0	10.6	4.3	6.3	6.71	.41	1.71	6.3	1.30	23	1	6
	1967		6.4	4.7	5.4	5.37	(.03)	.37	1.7	.40	18	1	11
Pediatrics	1966	5.5	12.5	4.0	6.0	7.69	1.69	2.19	8.5	.50	13	8	9
	1967		8.4	4.1	5.8	6.70	.90	1.20	4.3	.30	11	7	12
Hospitalwide	1966		7.0	5.3	6.28	6.25	(.03)	1.17	1.7	.60	22	3	5
Averages	1967		5.9	5.1	5.58	5.52	(.06)	.39	.8	.12	10	7	13

Days 'On Goal' are those where staffing varies less than 5 percent from goal. Example: 'On Goal' is range of 3.35–3.65, for goal of 3.5 hours.

to the success of the plan was—and is—the supervisor's explanation given when incentive checks are distributed. Without the explanation and ensuing discussion, much of the motivational value of the program disappears. That is what occurred in the laboratory, before the cause of the problem was isolated.

The first real fiasco occurred when Purchasing—to take advantage of volume buying—bought a full year's supply of a key laboratory item at one time. Due to a clerical error, the full year's cost was applied against the department's performances for one period, instead of the full year. The result on the incentive checks was devastating; and, without a correction or supervisory explanation, the failing went unnoticed (except by the employees). By coincidence, this took place during a very high activity period in which the formula should have produced substantial incentive payments. When the error was discovered employees received a makeup differential in a subsequent incentive check. However, that check arrived following a period of much lower activity; and, again, no supervisory explanation accompanied check distribution. Thus employees found little relationship between incentive pay and higher productivity. Without an explanation, it was small wonder that they lost faith in the program. The fact that overall payments averaged $30 to $40 per month meant little because credibility was gone. It took the hospital months of explanation to overcome this shortcoming; it also reemphasized to us the value of competent supervisory communications.

At the same time we introduced our first formulas in housekeeping and dietary services. Interestingly, both were hurried into being by peer pressure from employees who were witnessing the incentives paid in the Laundry. Also of interest was the reluctance of supervision in both departments to begin the programs, and a relative absence of scholarship on the hospital's part in developing the formulas.

At that time—1966—we were suffering through a period of relatively weak housekeeping supervision. But we had expanded the hospital area substantially, and some obvious opportunities to increase the value of production per employee existed. The first formula was primitive and lacked adequate historical data. It had to be adjusted soon after. But it is important to note that in this stage of our plan's development, the push for participation came from the employee, who saw something happening and wanted to share in it. The same can be said of Dietary. There we had a fine supervisor who in five years had generated real improvements, but incentives were new to her.

Finally, a look at Medical Records, which offers two comparisons of value. Here, we had excellent departmental direction from a supervisor who quickly grasped the concept and set about developing both historical data and realistic measuring devices. The department was already an efficiency pacemaker, and we were in a period of sharp statistical growth. Even so, once a plan was introduced there, we enjoyed significant reductions in both manhours and supplies, and morale became even better.

Under the formula, medical secretaries were compensated on the basis of lumping their productivity shares together and then allocating the dollars on the basis of the lines of dictation actually typed. It was an approach that was fair, and also encouraged maximum output.

Contrast our experience to what occurred in another hospital which hurried into a similar plan, but with two shortcomings: lack of a strong historical base and absence of a maximum limit on incentive pay. At the time their medical secretaries were earning about $300 monthly. When the plan was introduced in this department, staff was having difficulty handling transcribed dictation and were much behind in their work. Overcoming this was one of the points of urgency in hurrying the plan into being.

When dollar incentives linked to production were introduced, the secretaries amazed the hospital. One quickly tripled her output; the others doubled their production. The dictation bottleneck was soon dissolved, but now one secretary was earning nearly $1,000 a month and the other two over $500. This created a hospitalwide problem which soon forced the administration of that hospital to abandon the entire program.

Other examples were more obvious. Coffee Shop personnel and tray aides showed more concern for the patrons they served; maintenance people gave better attention to routine maintenance; on-call personnel responded more quickly; and the overall collection of statistical information moved with greater smoothness. Purchasing people developed a more critical understanding of cost values and inventory levels; and those responsible for tools, equipment, test processing, and even food preparation found in a very personal way that waste is a costly thing.

Perhaps it was best summed up in a conversation overheard one day between two housekeeping employees. The key line went this way: "From here on out, I'm watching *you!* I don't think you're doing your part around here and, the way I see it, that's costing *me* money!"

That says it all!

The plan was never intended as a substitute for good supervision or strong salary administration. It was designed to encourage people to work to their full capacities and to establish communications which drew employees together in a common bond. Some early critics felt that this method would have a short life; that once the "cream" had been skimmed from potential savings that results would falter. More than a decade of experience has demonstrated continuing positive effects.

Chapter 4

Others Came to Look

The experiments at Baptist Hospital were reaching many interested people by word of mouth. It was not an avalanche of interest, but slowly others were beginning to ask questions.

The incentive plan was still experimental when John Schill and I began to receive inquiries from other hospitals about our methods. There were invitations to speak, too, and requests for journal articles. To the former, we responded as affirmatively as we were able; but, since the concept was still evolving, we were reluctant to put much in writing.

At that stage, it was not easy to be too specific. The hospital had a concept, and management was doing its best to apply proven engineering and human relations principles. But mistakes were being made, and the whole plan was still largely experimental. Nevertheless, as month after month passed with growing success, communication began to develop.

The majority of requests were for an opportunity to have officials of other hospitals come to Pensacola to review what was being done and to see how it might be applicable elsewhere. At first these requests came once every few weeks; then the number climbed to once or twice weekly.

Although we were flattered, the flow of visitors was soon overwhelming. Having these guests come carved great gaps in our work schedules, for at that time there was no literature other than basic work sheets that could be shown to people. Thus, John Schill and I, with some help from involved department heads, would sit around for hours, sorting out approaches, trying to emphasize the important philosophical elements; then the group would try to aid the visitors in reaching some conclusions on how *they* might begin.

Everyone tried to be helpful, but after going through this a dozen times, it became obvious that we were achieving little. About then a

31

good friend, Marvin Altman of Fort Smith, Arkansas, came up with an idea.

Marvin had been one of our visitors and went back impressed with the potential. A few days later he called with a notebook full of unanswered questions. As we chatted, he commented:

> It seems to me there are lots of hospitals that should have this information—now. Why don't you fellows put together a workshop of, say, two or maybe three days? Put the program together with a classroom atmosphere, and I'll bet people will eat it up. I'll tell you what: if you'll produce the program, I'll organize the first class, here in Arkansas. We might even pay you for it!

It must have been that last sentence that got to me! So, that night Schill and I met with John Appleyard, our personnel consultant, and the three of us began putting a course together.

The big questions, of course, involved method and what disciplines should be involved from the hospitals. The three of us applied ourselves to the first point because experience had shown that the best way for people to understand what was being done was to make them struggle with the principles—digging out the details, plotting formula possibilities on paper, and drilling on the arithmetic.

Schill was the expert on this, and he also was the first to recognize from recent experience that some persons were slow to see the possibilities from a straight lecture presentation.

THE ARKANSAS SEMINAR

The course, which ultimately went through several revisions, began with an orientation that explained how the group would work and gave a background of how the plan had evolved in Pensacola. The springboard was a short slide film detailing some history of incentives in America and then setting forth principles as Baptist's management saw them. Then, in a four-hour discussion, goals were identified; John Schill reminisced on methods that had been used. I wound up that first session by illustrating some statistical results, including income to employees and savings to patients.

Then the conference body was divided into smaller groups, and each section (five or six persons) was assigned a series of written case studies, Harvard-style. Each study was written with the background of a departmental illustration from Baptist Hospital, sticking close to the actual story line.

The conferees then went to work, with Schill, Appleyard, and me guiding the discussions and helping each group work from known data to develop workable formulas. That first Arkansas meeting had about thirty enrollees, with from three to five representatives per hospital, who attacked the problems with real interest and (after a reasonable get acquainted period as a working group) became very effective. In the next day and a half, each group worked with five or six problems. In many cases, their ideas differed from what had been devised at Baptist.

With the problem-solving experience behind them, group members reassembled for a brief report on findings and a final session in which the three instructors tried to expose the class to other productivity ideas, sharing details of sick leave and retirement plans and programs borrowed from other hospitals. Also explained was Baptist's Employee Foundation, an ongoing internal "United Way," which gives the hospital a fair share approach to its community responsibilities, operated *in toto* by the employees themselves.

The Arkansas seminar was a huge success. Class members included administrators or assistants, business office heads, directors of nursing, and a variety of other department heads. That was to be the kind of mix drawn at the later conferences.

All were conducted at Pensacola (during winter months it is usually easier to get northerners to come to Florida) and drew attendance from Maine to the Rockies and several groups from Canada, including Canadian government officials anxious to promote efficiency within their national health program.

As the seminar approach continued, the hospital also had the privilege of entertaining specialists from other areas. One was J. J. Jehring, the late director of the University of Wisconsin's Center for the Study of Productivity Motivation, who returned many times and both gave and took from our program.

Others came from the Department of Health, Education, and Welfare, from the American Hospital Association, from *Hospitals* and *Modern Hospital* magazines, the *National Observer,* and other interested groups. See the Appendix for digests of four typical reports by these interested specialists.

Chapter 5

Readiness for Changes to Come

One lesson taught by association with productivity incentives has been that people, like universal conditions, change with the times. By that statement, I mean people generally—and people within a given institution. That is a fact of which we should not lose sight.

For example, when John Schill first proposed departmental incentive in our laundry, he knew that the terms of that incentive had to be both fair to all parties and easily comprehended by a work force totally unschooled in such things. To have begun by applying some form of universal, hospitalwide concept for reducing supply usage would have fallen not on deaf ears but on people who could not have followed the rationale or felt excitement for what was happening.

More than a decade later this has changed. Not that the employees are now engineers; but most *DO* follow the flow of incentive ideas now, and through experience they appreciate how they can participate and benefit. All of this makes it possible for the hospital to look ahead to a program with a far greater interrelationship of function than had been envisioned. Where once we felt that single departmental incentive plans were the only practical route, now we are on a new plateau of understanding—one on which many functions can interrelate on supply consumption or those other areas where commonality exists. Where once there were jurisdictional disputes over supply consumption, now we have come of age and can review matters as an entity.

This is fortunate, for who knows how long hospitals will face the continuing supply cost formula? Who can judge the manner in which individual disciplines might be altered by regionalization? Who can imagine what future changes are in store through technology?

Every incentive formula is vulnerable to these things, but the more unusual the practices can be made, the more flexible they become, and the greater will be the hospital's ability to adjust and keep a program meaningful. This was the goal when Medicus engineers were engaged to add factors of simplicity and equity to our formulas and to seek an accommodation with criticism involving quality. This was the charge given to Jim Hicks and Ernest Williamson in 1974 when the revamping began. Part Two of this book details that program.

THE INTERVENING YEARS

I have not tried to examine all of the experiments or to report results in all departments. What has been illustrated should be an adequate preface, and the statistical tables and graphs in the Appendices provide the documentation. By early 1967 the program was achieving significant results and had outgrown informal supervision. By now, close to 80 percent of our employees were covered in departmental programs and, though appreciation of the results was not universal, most employees, a majority of our physicians, and others who came to inspect the results found much to their liking.

We had reached some conclusions, too, based on experience. It was apparent that we could profit from a staff industrial engineer to monitor and update formulas as conditions warranted. The hospital had utilized consulting industrial engineers for specific studies and had found them generally helpful, although in some instances there had been employee resistance to this work. Now, it seemed that more specific skills might be applied systematically. The effort was made, but it proved unsuccessful. Just why the engineer failed is still difficult to pin down. He had a fine background; but, as the next two years evolved, there was an apparent difference between his aptitudes and the hospital's needs. The monitoring and improved work standards we had hoped for failed to materialize; ultimately he left by mutual agreement.

Then in rapid order, four events took place that forced productivity incentives into a subordinate position from which they did not emerge for more than five years.

First came the hospital's acquisition of the Hillhaven Convalescent Center, a four-story nursing home adjacent to the general hospital. Converted to the Specialty Care Center, this facility placed a heavy demand on hospital management and support personnel, creating a work overload that robbed specialists of time that might have been applied to incentives.

Second, the influence of the severe nationwide inflation began to be felt, and this had a dramatic effect on incentive formulas. By 1969 the threats were a reality; and, without strong programs in supervision, it was impossible to keep formulas based on supply units and their costs current. Our original simple concepts were created in a period of relative price stability; by the end of the decade, it was almost impossible to sustain such formulas.

The third intervening factor was an upcoming building program. In early 1969 after several years of active planning, construction began on a $6 million expansion. Both John Schill and I were heavily committed to these details and also to plans for the first capital funds campaign in twenty years. Supervision of incentives slipped still further.

As all this happened, we were advised of a pending Internal Revenue Service regulation that could possibly jeopardize the tax-exempt status of hospitals engaging in "profit sharing plans." At this point, it was impossible to judge where the Baptist Hospital plan might stand in the light of such a ruling (this will be discussed fully in Chapter 6). Understandingly, this, too, had a negative effect on the hospital's pursuit of its incentives program.

To climax this series of negative influences, John Schill decided to enter private business. This alone would have been a serious setback; coupled with others, it literally forced the hospital to place incentives on a back burner. But the fact that the program not only survived but continued to prosper is testimony, we believe, to the validity of the productivity incentive concept for hospitals. The disappointment was in the fact that although formulas were sustained and updated, little of the sophistication we had hoped for was introduced. Yet with all these negative forces, the plan *did* survive, and its cost-controlling influence continued to be felt even in the face of double-digit inflation. As the intervening years passed, the funds campaign and building program were successfully completed, the long legal negotiation with the IRS was won, and somehow the emphasis on productivity and cost control was maintained, even in the face of growing employee concern over salary levels, quality of care, Occupational Safety and Health Administration (OSHA) regulations, and the host of other problems confronting hospitals in the early and mid-1970s.

Then Medicus joined us, and a reconcentration began. But that is the theme for Part Two of this book.

Chapter 6

Incentives and the Internal Revenue Service

When the incentive program went into effect in 1965, none of us gave any thought to a possible conflict with federal tax codes. We were, after all, a tax-exempt organization; and the end result of the plan was to reduce costs, hold down charges to patients, and reward employees for their roles in controlling manhours worked and supply utilization.

During the first six years of the plan's life there were frequent communications with Don Carner at Long Beach Memorial Medical Center concerning the Merit Plan, that hospital's group incentive, and with other institutions that had employed some form of financial motivation program. In each instance management viewed the efforts as positive in the public good.

Then, in the spring of 1972, tremors caused concern and response.

Word began to circulate that the Internal Revenue Service was taking a new look at incentive or profit-sharing programs in tax-exempt institutions. At first the reports were fragmented, but they carried enough weight to generate followup. As a result, correspondence was opened with Robert S. Bromberg, a Cleveland attorney and former regulations specialist for IRS. Bromberg was then both attorney and consultant in cases related to IRS regulations.

Bromberg shortly reported that there was indeed a reversal in time-honored IRS policies stemming from a case involving the Ohio Christian Church. Quoting from Bromberg's letter of transmittal: ". . . . . it (the ruling) may be interpreted as prohibiting any type of cost sharing plan which results in the distribution of some part of the profits to employees IN ANY FASHION. . . . "

According to hospital philosophy, the incentive plan did not involve "profits" but cost savings, and the plan was not "profit sharing" but an effort to control costs. The IRS ruling, however, appeared to be zeroing in on any form of institutional funds distribution that differed from conventional wage and salary or pension programming. Bromberg suggested that Baptist Hospital might wish to join with others using similar plans and initiate a high level conference with the IRS to obtain a review.

Naturally, that action began at once.

We prepared an in-depth brief of the program history, including formulas, methods, and sums paid. Other hospitals, including Don Carner's, followed suit. A letter of parallel explanation was sent to our Congressman, Robert L. F. Sikes, asking for his assistance in initiating the conference.

Then began two years of letters, questions, analysis, and inquiry as the Revenue Service, in its orderly manner, probed the basis of the incentive plan and its impact on health care.

At this point, it is only fair to acknowledge the painstaking role Mr. Bromberg introduced into this scenario. Because he had a broad background in the workings of the IRS, he knew the right way to proceed and promptly secured, always through the proper channels, interim conferences to help sustain a proper perspective for our type of institution and program. After each of these, his reports to the hospital were detailed and filled with additional requests for information on program implementation. For example, as late as May, 1974, he would write:

> ... they have also inquired as to how the program is communicated to the employees, that is, what documents are furnished to the employees to advise them of the formula on which their shares in the program are based. The Service also has inquired as to the document of written instrument which spells out the 25 percent hospitalwide sharing formula for the plan. Please send such an instrument, a resolution of your Board of Trustees approving it, or at least an adequate description of how this formula is arrived at and has been communicated to your employees. In general, as you can see, the Service would like some concrete written document which more adequately defines the workings of your program, and that established the formulas of benefits. ...

As negotiations proceeded, the Service identified sections of our plan that authorities felt were not consistent with the spirit of new interpretations of the law. As these were identified, the hospital took corrective action and removed or revised the offending portions. One example was in the Coffee Shop. Responding to a written IRS statement, Bromberg had replied:

> With respect to the Hospitality Shop (Coffee Shop), Baptist Hospital agrees that the basis for the formula measuring payment into its incentive program should not be based upon net income. At present they are developing a formula under which the payment would come from tips provided by customers receiving satisfactory service. This would provide the employees with performance goals and permit payment based on public satisfaction. . . .

In another instance, negotiations climaxed with this statement: "With respect to the Speech and Hearing Department, the hospital agrees that the formula should *not* be based on department income. . . . " This came after nearly twenty-four months of presentation in which the individual formulas had been sent forth, along with detailed descriptions of how the plan had originated and been revised, and of how benefits had accrued to patients as well as staff.

As these negotiations were in progress there was also work in progress before the Congress to amend tax laws specifically with regard to our and similar measures. Consequently, Mr. Bromberg, with input from the several interested hospitals, prepared a fifteen-page brief for presentation before the House Ways and Means Committee. That brief, plus another dozen pages of exhibits, helped assure that there would be no legislation opposed to the institutional productivity incentive in the tax-exempt institution.

One by one, points at issue were resolved. On August 1, 1974, the hospital received a three-page letter written July 29 (Exhibit 6–1) and signed by Milton Cerny, Chief, Ruling Section 1, Exempt Organizations Branch.

And so, subject to limitations acceptable to Baptist Hospital, the plan received clearance to proceed. That was a happy day! But the ruling was not universal. It applied only to *our* plan; and, at the time of this writing, the Baptist Hospital productivity incentive program is the only one with IRS approval. This was the "green light" the plan needed to move into a new phase where lessons from prior experience could be updated in a renewal of interest.

The IRS examination was not a simple test; the two years of examination forced the hospital to satisfy federal regulations; it also forced staff to review goals and methods. It was the perfect springboard to the future.

Department of the Treasury

AUG   1 1974

Internal Revenue Service
Washington, DC 20224

Date: JUL 29 1974 | In reply refer to: T:MS:EO:R:1-1

DO 59
EIN 59-0657322

▷   Baptist Hospital
c/o Pat N. Groner
1000 West Moreno Street
Pensacola, Florida   32501

Gentlemen:

This is in reply to your request for a ruling whether the operation of your Productivity-Incentive Program will adversely affect your tax exempt status under section 501(c)(3) of the Internal Revenue Code.

Our records show that you have been recognized as exempt from Federal income tax under section 501(c)(3) of the Code.

You have indicated that the program was established in 1965 and has primarily been operated on a department-by-department basis. The purposes of the program are to increase productivity in manpower and the use of supplies, lower costs and charges, eliminate overtime and maintain the highest quality of care.

This program is limited to employees and supervisory personnel, such as nursing supervisors and department heads. Management personnel, such as the hospital administrator, do not participate. Neither do any of the physicians or hospital-based specialists.

The basic thrust of the program is to apply appropriate standards of measurement to the quality and quantity of the services performed by employees in order to reward them for any measurable increases in productivity. Wherever possible the components of the formulas used to compute the compensation paid to employees under the program are limited to controllable items of expense and no employees whose achievement does not exceed a reasonable predetermined standard of general acceptability is permitted to share in the supplemental compensation of the department for any given calendar quarter. All compensation under the program is paid to employees on a quarterly basis and no portion is deferred by being deposited in any pension or profit sharing trust.

The productivity formula for each department attempts to measure increased productivity. These formulae are generally based upon a savings of either manhours or supplies, or some combination of both. In a few cases, the quality of the services provided, which is measured by patient or customer satisfaction, is the only basis for making the determinations. All formulae involving comparisons of dollar costs include provision for making appropriate adjustments to reflect price changes. The formulae also universally contain maximums for individual shares to insure that the compensation paid is reasonable and that the Hospital will be the main beneficiary of all economies resulting from the operation of the program. Another purpose for setting limitations on the amount of individual compensation payable is that you have attempted to keep the remuneration high enough to encourage efforts toward increased efficiency, but not so high as to generate neglect of the patient's welfare. The current maximum individual share is $50 per month.

It is our understanding that the program has been, and will be, periodically revised.

Based on the information submitted, we have concluded that your productivity-incentive program will not affect your exempt status so long as the cost savings under the program do not adversely interfere with the quality or quantity of care rendered to patients. Our conclusion is also based on the understanding that your productivity formulae do not, and will not utilize net income, gross receipts, or other factors which bear no relation to productivity or efficiency of employees in computing employee benefits under the program.

Sincerely yours,

Milton Cerny
Chief, Rulings Section 1
Exempt Organizations Branch

Part Two

Chapter 7

Development and Design

Recently, someone asked me how many hospitals actually installed Baptist's method and how long they used it. I cannot give a complete answer. Many who attended our seminars introduced incentives in at least part of their hospitals; some, I understand, still have departmental programs in progress, with continuing good results. Some (including my brother, who has managed Baptist Memorial Hospital in Memphis for many years) do not agree with the method.

Some expressed belief that the method would last only temporarily and would fade with dimming employee interest. Others could not agree to a commitment to employees which would extend beyond a given year. In any event, I did not maintain thorough communication with others who had visited us, though I have often wished I had.

Our program continued! In the decade of its existence, many things have been done to update and maintain it. Admittedly, it has had certain ups and downs, largely due to the need for administration to focus on other major national problems, such as those imposed by Medicare, inflation, and the technical revolution. Today, however, the program is moving into a new era, stronger than ever—and more relevant. That is what the succeeding chapters are about. For this work, the hospital employed the professional services of The Medicus Systems Corporation, represented by Management Engineers Jim Hicks and Ernest Williamson. I am grateful to them both for their expertise and workmanlike, farsighted approach, and for their assistance in developing materials for the next chapters. John Schill had left when their work was done; the hospital had passed through a long building program; and our incentive plan had been challenged by the Internal Revenue Service (after two years, IRS gave the plan its full blessing, the only such ruling to date).

Thus, the incentive program, without a true helmsman for many months, was in serious need of revamping.

Revitalizing the Employee Productivity Incentive Program for Baptist meant incorporation of many basic concepts from the original program—plus a new degree of sophistication and a stronger emphasis on quality. Some elements of the original program that had caused difficulties were revised; those that had produced the greatest successes were maintained. The revitalized plan was to introduce a new sophistication which time, experience, and circumstances permitted; its design included motivating personnel to become active members of a team that will profit from past lessons and adopt new ones to promote both quality and efficiency.

PHILOSOPHY

Jim Hicks and Ernest Williamson did not alter the philosophy of the plan. They began with the belief that both patients and hospital employees could benefit if Baptist could fulfill its mission of providing quality care through more effective utilization of resources. Studies showed that employee incentive concepts used successfully in other industries would motivate hospital personnel to function more productively.

Restudying the past reconfirmed that everyone must benefit to assure the success of an incentive plan. Patients must receive quality care at a fair cost, employees must receive additional income and appropriate recognition for contributions beyond the norm, and the hospital should generate increased funds for its patient needs.

PURPOSE AND OBJECTIVES

In an effort not to alter the past philosophy or emphasis of the incentive program, the goal was to structure the plan as an employee benefit that paid employees a monetary reward for exceptional productivity and goal accomplishment.

Restudying the plan, three basic objectives were confirmed:

1. To motivate personnel to reduce costs through improved utilization of manpower and supplies.
2. To ensure that quality of patient care is maximized.
3. To reward personnel when utilization of manpower and supplies has resulted in increased productivity while maintaining a high level of quality in the provision of patient care.

Other specifics were established as follows:

1. To develop cost consciousness in each employee.
2. To effect greater control on the use of supplies and other hospital resources.
3. To encourage new ideas of improved methods, equipment, and services.
4. To recognize financial and psychological needs of employees with rewards for increased productivity and quality service.
5. To provide a benefit which will aid in recruitment and retention of personnel.
6. To assure the patient an affordable level of quality care.

Inherent in these objectives was the idea that the incentive plan should motivate personnel to become participating and innovative members of a team dedicated to a common goal.

All these goals created difficulties for, in a sense, they were shifting certain gears from one plan to another. Involved also were some new and complex ideas that required careful explanation and maintenance.

To accomplish the objectives, the revised plan had to incorporate several nonsimilar elements with counterbalancing emphasis. The utilization of employee time is measured in the Manpower Utilization Program by comparing actual manpower used per unit of output to an established standard. The utilization of supplies is measured in the Supply Utilization Program by comparing actual usage per an appropriate consumption factor (items/patient units) versus a standard established from actual historical usage. These two programs provide a measurement of effectiveness assuming that the quality of service being rendered remains at an acceptable level. To assure that unacceptable quality levels do not result, each department manager must establish quality guidelines for his area of responsibility. These Quality Assurance Programs can range from very sophisticated, highly developed, and statistically sound formal programs (which generate objective, definable evaluations) to purely subjective appraisals. The level of objectivity for these programs depends on the nature of the service being rendered by the department, the degree to which quality is quantifiable, and the cost of collecting quality information. The ultimate decision relative to quality control objectivity and costs is made by the hospital's assistant director who has responsiblity for the given department.

The Manpower and Supply Utilization programs each compare actual performance against established standards; and, if standards are met through efficient operations, a dollar amount of savings is calculated.

The savings from the Manpower Utilization Program from any department are distributed 70 percent to departmental employees and 30 percent to a hospitalwide pool, which also receives the savings from the Supply Utilization Program. Deductions are made for overtime or unacceptable quality. Of equal importance to the distribution of incentive award checks was development of performance ratings for each department. These ratings were calculated periodically and provided continuous feedback to each department indicating levels of efficiency.

The Manpower and Supply Programs were intended to encourage personnel to sharpen cost consciousness; the Quality Assurance Programs ensured that increased productivity did not occur at the expense of quality. The combination of feedback on progress, quality, and quarterly sharing of the savings generated by these efforts were expected to encourage continuing performance improvement. Thus, our new approach is a refinement of the old, but not a radical departure.

That represents the basic skeleton of the new Employee Productivity Incentive Plan. Now a look behind the frontispiece.

Chapter 8

Manpower Utilization Program

The new Manpower Utilization Program compares actual levels of manpower usage to specified standard levels of usage. Here the word *standard* refers to the time determined as necessary for a qualified worker to complete a defined amount of work of specified quality while working a normal pace under capable supervision and experiencing normal fatigue and delays. Standards used for these comparisons were established for each department based on engineering methods, past history, national comparisons, and detailed interviews.

Each standard was expressed in terms of a specified number of worked manhours for an appropriate workload unit. The term *manhour* is a unit for measuring work equivalent to one man working sixty minutes or two men working for thirty minutes, or some similar combination of men working for a period of time. The term *workload* refers to the measure established in a particular department for defining the volume or level of work or production in that department. For instance, typical standards might take the form of manhours per patient day, or manhours per procedure, or manhours per 100 pounds of clean linen processed.

TARGET AND REWARD LEVELS

In the new plan, the hospital established two standard levels for each department, labeled the Target Level and the Reward Level. The Target Level is a number representing a level of performance attainable and desirable for the department. The Reward Level is by definition 10 percent looser than the Target Level and represents both the least accept-

51

able level at which a department should perform and the level at which incentive rewards commence. More specifically, these two terms reflect:

Target Level: The Target Level is the standard of personnel performance that reflects the work pace of a motivated worker with sufficient skill and capability, performing a specified task under capable supervision. This number includes normal fatigue and delay time and represents a pace that can be maintained without harmful effect on the worker or the quality of his work.

Reward Level: The Reward Level is the standard of performance that reflects the work pace established by management as being acceptable. The Reward Level is set 10 percent higher than the Target Level and is the level at which incentive rewards commence.

In this plan, both the Target Level and the Reward Level are now expressed in terms of Manhours Per Workload Unit. The hospital recognizes several classifications of hours, including worked hours, paid hours, and other hours. *Worked hours* are of primary importance to the Manpower Utilization Program and are referred to as manhours. Included in these hours are all productive time, that is, regular worked hours and overtime worked hours. *Paid hours,* on the other hand, include all time for which the employee is paid. This term includes worked hours, sick hours, vacation, and holiday hours. Time included in paid hours but not actually definable as worked hours, is *other hours.* Two other classifications referred to in the Manpower Utilization Program are earned hours and saved hours. *Earned hours* are determined by using either the Target Level or the Reward Level as the reference base. In most calculations of this program, unless otherwise specified, earned hours are the hours necessary to complete a specified level of workload by working at the pace defined by the Reward Level. *Saved hours* represent the difference between earned hours and worked hours (earned minus worked equals saved).

The development of standards for each cost center involved a series of steps that varied for each cost unit. The procedure in developing standards included these steps:

Step 1. An interview with the department head to discuss the department's activities, role, workload, and statistical reports.

Step 2. Studies to determine the most appropriate measure of workload (e.g., patient days or square footage).

Step 3. The collection of data on historical operations in each depart-

ment in accord with units of workload measurement established in
Step 2.

Step 4. An analysis of present operations to ascertain recent changes
or developments.

Step 5. Studies to determine time requirements for major procedures
(if not all) performed in each department.

Step 6. Conversion of these procedure times into overall departmental standards in terms of worked manhours per workload unit.

Step 7. A comparison of these standards to those of other similar
hospitals (when possible), and a review with the department head.

Step 8. Development of the Target Level for each cost center or department.

Step 9. A fine tuning of the Target Level after comparing to historical
data and a review with department heads.

Step 10. Development of the Reward Level for each cost center once
the Target Level is established.

Step 11. Development of workload counting and reporting mechanisms.

Although Baptist when surveyed had 107 cost centers, there were only
73 responsibility centers. Because of the combining of cost centers only
73 departmental standards were required. Table 8-1 lists departments
for which development of standards was required with the associated
cost center numbers and units of workload.

Table 8-1 Departmental Workload Measures

Department	Cost Center(s)	Workload Units
Nursing Administration	600	100 patient days
Medical I	610	Patient days for the unit
Medical II	612	Patient days for the unit
Surgical I	614	Patient days for the unit
Surgical II	616	Patient days for the unit
Orthopedics	618	Patient days for the unit
Eye Unit	620	Patient days for the unit
Neurology	622	Patient days for the unit

Table 8-1 (Continued)

Department	Cost Center(s)	Workload Units
Genito-Urinary	624	Patient days for the unit
Pediatrics	630	Patient days for the unit
Obstetrics/Gynecology	646	Patient days for the unit
Nursery	650	Nursery days for the unit
Medical Intensive Nursing Unit	640	Patient days for the unit
Surgical Intensive Nursing Unit	641	Patient days for the unit
Intensive Coronary Care Unit	642	Patient days for the unit
Delivery	670	Deliveries
Emergency Services	678, 679	Patients seen
Central Supply Room	676	Patient days
Drug Room	732	100 weighted procedures
Renal Dialysis	746	Procedures
Nursing Administration, SCC*	601	100 patient days
Skilled Nursing Facility	611, 613	Patient days for the unit
Mental Health Unit	643	Patient days for the unit
Alcohol Intervention Unit	645	Patient days for the unit
Central Supply Room, SCC	675	Patient days for the unit
Drug Administration Pharmacy, SCC	731	100 medications administered
Operating Suite	660	OR hours in use

*SCC—Specialty Care Center (the hospital's extended care building, including the Mental Health Unit).

Table 8-1 (Continued)

Department	Cost Center(s)	Workload Units
Recovery Room	666	Patient hours
Anesthesia	735	Weighted procedures
Pharmacy	730	100 line items
Physical Therapy	737, 739	100 weighted procedures
Occupational Therapy	738	Procedures
Speech and Hearing	744	Procedures
Respiratory Therapy	736, 749	100 weighted procedures
Laboratory	702, 703 706, 707 705, 715	100 weighted procedures
Electrodiagnostics	712, 713	100 weighted procedures
Gastroenterology Lab	718	100 weighted procedures
Radiology	721, 723 724, 726 727, 728	100 weighted procedures
Radiation Therapy	722	100 weighted procedures
Oncology	729	100 weighted procedures
Pulmonary Lab	748	100 weighted procedures
Food Service	800, 810	Weighted dietary services
Food Service, SCC	801	Weighted dietary services
Hospitality Shop	854	Units sold
Laundry Services	860, 864	100 clean linen pounds
Housekeeping Services	850, 851	1000 square feet cleaned
Grounds	838, 839	1000 weighted square yards
Plant, Maintenance	830, 831 834, 835	1000 square feet

Table 8-1 (Continued)

Department	Cost Center(s)	Workload Units
Electronics Maintenance	836	Weighted pieces of equipment
Professional Office Building	112	1000 square feet
Purchasing	955	Number of department charges
Print Shop	880	Final copies
Administration	950	100 patient days
Administration, SCC	951	Patient days
Fiscal Services	900	Admissions
Admitting	920	Weighted admissions
Credit	934	100 weighted procedures
Admitting/Credit, SCC	935	Weighted admissions and discharges
Cashier	930	Weighted Discharges and receipts
Emergency Associates	875	Physician Visits
Payroll/Accounting	902	Checks issued
Data Processing	936	Patient days
Communications	937	Patient days
Pastoral Care	957	100 weighted consultations
Development	962	100 patient days
Patient Representatives	970	Patient days
Gift Shop	855	100 dollars in sales
Personnel	952	Employees
Education	954	Employees

Table 8-1 (Continued)

Department	Cost Center(s)	Workload Units
TV Rental	857	Rental days
Medical Records	768	100 weighted procedures
Medical Library	769	100 patient days
University of West Florida Health Center	111	Patients seen

HISTORICAL DATA CONTRIBUTION

Once cost centers were aligned with the departments and workload units were defined, collection of historical data began for each department. It was important that the quantities of workload, such as numbers of procedures, pounds of laundry, or patient days, be ascertained for approximately the preceding twelve months. In some cases there were multiple sources for data. (For example, the quantity of patient days was available from a Medical Records report, a Nursing Office report, and the Data Processing census report.) Because these reports were prepared in a different manner at different times of the day and for different purposes, the number of patient days on these reports seldom agreed. Therefore, it became important that the exact source of each workload unit be specified before standards were set. Ultimately there were twenty-nine data sources:

1. Labor Distribution Report
2. Patient Revenue Usage and Statistical Report
3. Census Summary Report
4. Analysis of Hospital Services/Medical Statistical Report
5. Monthly Narrative Report, Nursing Division
6. Monthly Activity Report, Emergency Room
7. Monthly Surgical Report
8. Anesthesia Report
9. Monthly Laboratory Report
10. Monthly Electrodiagnostics Report (EEG/EKG)
11. Monthly Gastroenterology Lab Report

12. Monthly X-Ray Report
13. Monthly Statistical Report, Pulmonary Services
14. Monthly Physical Therapy Report
15. Monthly Occupational Therapy Report
16. Monthly Speech and Hearing Report
17. Monthly Pharmacy Report
18. Monthly Dietary Report
19. Monthly Hospitality Shop Report
20. Monthly Laundry and Linen Report
21. Monthly Purchasing/Print Shop Report
22. Monthly Building Services Report
23. Monthly Fiscal Services Report
24. Monthly Payroll/Accounting Report
25. Monthly Personnel Activity Report
26. Monthly Medical Records Report
27. Monthly Chaplain's Report
28. Monthly Volunteer Services Report
29. Monthly T.V. Rental Report

The majority of these sources were in existence when this project began. However, it was necessary to establish new monthly reports for proper reporting of activities of the Hospitality Shop, Purchasing/Print Shop, Building Services, Fiscal Services, Payroll/Accounting, Medical Records, Volunteer Services, and TV Rental. Workload statistics for most of these areas were being maintained within the department but were not recorded on any regular basis.

With sources defined, the third requirement was assembly of historical data to determine actual levels of performance for the prior twelve months for use in building standards. For example, it was important that the number of Worked Manhours Per Patient Day be determined for each nursing unit for each of the twelve preceding months. (The period used in this analysis was from October, 1973, through September, 1974.) An example of the worksheet used to collect this data is shown in Exhibit 8-1. Several other pieces of pertinent data were included on this worksheet. If comparative data were available from either Hospital Administrative Services reports or similar institutions, it was introduced. The number of Authorized Skill Levels was also assembled, and the equivalent authorized worked manhours per standardized workload unit was calculated.

The consultants recognized, of course, that caution had to be exercised when the performance level of this hospital was compared with that of other hospitals or even Hospital Administrative Services (HAS) data. For example, the HAS report lists "laundry pounds per manhour,"

Exhibit 8-1

DEPT. (C.C. NO.) ●
WORKLOAD UNITS ●
SOURCE ●

TARGET ●	REWARD ●

HISTORICAL DATA OCT. 1973 - MAR. 1975				COMPARATIVE DATA
MO.	MANHRS.	WORKLD.	INDEX	
O				
N				
D				
Q1				
J				
F				
M				
Q2				AUTHORIZED SKILL LEVELS
A				
M				
J				
Q3				
J				
A				
S				
Q4				
O				
N				
D				
Q1				REMARKS
J				
F				
M				
Q2				

ANAL.	073-S74	073-M75
AVERAGE		
MINIMUM		
MEDIAN		
MAXIMUM		

DATE EFFECTIVE ●	APPROVED BY ●

as the productivity indicator for laundry services. The manhours used in HAS reports are "paid manhours," and the workload unit is "soiled laundry processed," excluding any extended care facility usage. When an indicator is calculated using *these* statistics, it is significantly different from an index generated by using "worked manhours" and "pounds of clean linen issued" as manhour statistics and workload units. Thus, any time comparisons were made with data from other facilities, consideration was given to its relevance and its validity at Baptist Hospital. In a number of cases, the nature of comparative data was known and could be adjusted to minimize the differences.

REVIEW OF PRESENT OPERATIONS

With an analysis of historical trends completed, the present operations of each department were reviewed. In those departments where definable procedures were performed, time requirements for these procedures were determined. For example, in Radiology there are 124 different procedures on the catalog. By timing those frequently performed procedures and obtaining best estimates of time requirements for those less frequently performed, a set of time requirements was established for all procedures. Times were compared to predetermined time standards, which were available from other similar studies. In Radiology, requirements expressed in minutes spent actually performing the procedures provided standards such as these:

Procedure	Minutes
Chest, PA only	5.0
Rib, bilateral	14.0
Lumbosacral spine	12.0
Humerus	9.0
IVP	60.0
GI and GE	22.0
Nephrotomogram	95.0

Once the time requirements for the procedures performed in any one department were determined, a standard was established for that department. This standard was reviewed, analyzed, and compared with other standards and historical trends for accuracy and eventually fine tuned into a measurement of the desired performance of that department referred to as the Target Level. The Target Level was similarly determined for all hospital departments. From this Target Level, another standard was generated—referred to as the Reward Level. As stated earlier, the Reward Level is a level of performance set approximately 10 percent looser than the Target Level. This standard was set to provide an acceptable level at which incentive pay can commence below the optimal Target Level.

Once standards were established, the engineers defined the system to compare actual performance with established standard levels of performance. This was done to provide a logical, understandable means for determining efficiencies, for calculating savings of manhours and dollars, and for providing us with a continuing feedback on each department's progress toward improved labor utilization.

ACTUAL LEVEL OF PERFORMANCE

Just as it is possible to specify a Target Level or a Reward Level, it is possible by knowing actual manhours and workload in a period to calculate the actual level of performance. The *actual level*, which is sometimes referred to as the *productivity index*, is that ratio of manhours to workload actually observed in a particular period. The actual level is expressed in terms comparable with those terms used for expressing the Target Level and the Reward Level.

As the new plan evolves, there are two major manpower utilization calculations made during or at the end of each quarter for each department. One is the determination of the performance rating, or efficiency of the department. The *performance rating* is the ratio of standard (or target) time to actual time. More specifically, the performance rating, expressed as a percentage, we calculate by the formula:

$$\text{Percentage Performance Rating} = \frac{\text{Target Level} \times 100}{\text{Actual Level}}$$

This rating is calculated at the end of each month of the quarter, and then a composite rating is calculated at the end of the quarter to express overall efficiency of the department for the quarter.

The other of the two major calculations is the determination of dollars saved by the department due to the efficient use of manpower. This is achieved by multiplying the saved hours by the average hourly wage index for that department. The *average hourly wage index* represents the average hourly wage of persons in a specified department and is calculated from payroll records by dividing the total regular dollar earnings by the total regular hours worked for the department. This wage index is calculated at the beginning of the quarter, and its value is applied to saved hours each month to determine dollar savings from manpower efficiencies.

In case all of this is getting a little deep, it might help to try a little practical experiment and review.

Thus far, we have discussed new terms, including target level, reward level, actual level, manhours, workload units, earned hours, worked hours, saved hours, percentage performance rating, average hourly wage index, and dollars saved. The relationships among these concepts, and calculations involving them, will become clear in an example.

MANPOWER UTILIZATION PROGRAM CALCULATIONS

Let's assume we are examining a medical nursing unit's manpower performance during a quarter. Productivity indices, or levels of performance, are measured in terms of manhours per patient day. Assume that the established manpower standards for this department are as follows:

> Target Level: 4.05 manhours per patient day
> Reward Level: 4.46 manhours per patient day

Note that the Reward Level, the level at which incentive rewards commence, was set at a level 10 percent looser than Target (Target 4.05 + 0.41 = Reward 4.46), thereby in this case allowing for 0.41 manhours more per patient day than the 4.05 manhours per patient day specified by the Target Level. Suppose that the Census Summary Report shows that there were *1300* patient days on that medical nursing unit for the first month of the period and that during that same month Payroll records show that hours on that unit were as follows:

Regular	5200 Hours
Overtime	200 Hours
Sick and Other	56 Hours

By definition, manhours equals worked hours, which equals regular hours plus overtime hours. Therefore, manhours for the month were *5400* (5200 regular plus 200 overtime).

Knowing the actual manhours and actual patient days, we can calculate the actual level or actual productivity index by the following method:

$$\text{Actual level} = 4.15 \text{ manhours per patient day} = \frac{5400 \text{ manhours}}{1300 \text{ patient days}}$$

At this point, the following factors are known:

Target Level	4.05 manhours per patient day
Reward Level	4.46 manhours per patient day
Actual Level	4.15 manhours per patient day
* Manhours	5400 manhours
* Patient Days	1300 patient days

Note that although the nursing unit has not reached the maximum effective level of performance specified by the Target Level, the department has displayed a degree of efficiency by surpassing the Reward Level. The exact efficiency or percentage performance rating is calculated by comparing actual to target or, more specifically, by the following calculation:

$$\text{Percentage performance rating} = \frac{4.05 \text{ target}}{4.15 \text{ actual}} \times 100 = 97.6$$

To calculate the savings in hours represented by this level of efficiency, it is necessary to know earned hours and worked hours. Worked hours were 5400. Earned hours are determined by multiplying the Reward Level times the actual patient days, as follows:

Earned hours = 5798 hours = 4.46 reward manhours
per patient day x 1300 patient days

It is easy now to calculate saved hours by subtracting worked hours from earned hours:

Saved hours = 398 hours = (5798 earned hours − 5400
worked hours)

Assuming that the average hourly wage index is $4.00, as determined from Payroll records, these 398 saved hours represent $1,592.00 saved dollars (398 saved hours x $4.00 per hour).

Thus the calculation can be summarized as follows:

Target Level	4.05 MH/Pd *
Reward Level	4.46 MH/Pd
Worked Hours	5400 MH
Patient Days	1300 Pd
Actual Level	4.15 MH/Pd

* MH = manhours; Pd = patient day

Earned Hours	5798 MH
Worked Hours	5400 MH
Saved Hours	398 MH
Average Hourly Wage Index	$4.00 MH
Dollars Saved	$1592
Performance Rating	97.6%

Suppose that in the following month in the same department worked hours equaled 5550 and patient days equaled 1220. These same calculations would yield the following results:

Target Level	4.05 MH/Pd
Reward Level	4.46 MH/Pd
Worked Hours	5550 MH
Patient Days	1220 Pd
Actual Level	4.55 MH/Pd
Earned Hours	5441 MH
Worked Hours	5550 MH
Saved Hours	(109) MH
Average Hourly	
Wage Index	$4.00 MH
Dollars Saved	$(436)
Performance Rating	89.0%

Note that the actual level is higher than the Reward Level, that worked hours are greater than earned hours, yielding a deficit in saved hours and dollars saved, and that efficiency is below 90 percent, or the minimum acceptable level. There is administrative recognition of this inefficiency through a reporting of all monthly performance ratings to the administration.

Next, suppose that the following and final month of the quarter the department performed at a level better than both the Reward and the Target Level, and that calculations yielded the following results:

Target Level	4.05 MH/Pd
Reward Level	4.46 MH/Pd
Worked Hours	5200 MH
Patient Days	1300 Pd

Actual Level	$4.00 MH/Pd
Earned Hours	5798 MH
Worked Hours	5200 MH
Saved Hours	598 MH
Average Hourly Wage Index	4.00/MH
Dollars Saved	$2392
Performance Rating	101.3%

Note that the department performed at a level of 101.3 percent efficiency, that is, at a level surpassing the Target Level. It is not inconceivable that occasionally a department might perform at levels better than target; however, consistent performance at these levels usually implies that some major factor has changed in such a way as to make revision of the standard necessary. It is important to note that the Manpower Utilization Program monitors performance ratings in a continuing manner, pinpointing not only inefficient departments but also those departments where efficiency has significantly improved, possibly to the point where review of standards is warranted.

At this point, we can summarize the performance of the nursing unit throughout the quarter as shown in Table 8-2.

There are several important points to note with respect to this summary. First, the actual level for the quarter, 4.23 manhours per patient day, is a composite of the quarter's activity and is computed by dividing total worked hours by total patient days for the quarter. Second, the performance rating for the quarter is also a composite figure calculated by dividing the Target Level by the composite actual level for the quarter (this is the figure 95.7 percent in the column marked Total). And third, the sum of the dollars saved for the quarter equaled $3,548.00.

The process illustrated in the example is similar to those following for each department during each quarter. Data are gathered from specified sources to determine manhour and workload levels for each department. The calculations of performance ratings and dollars saved are also performed monthly. At the end of each month and at the end of the quarter reports specifying performance ratings by department are distributed to appropriate management personnel for review. Dollars saved are calculated at the end of each quarter and are allocated 70 percent to the departmental pool and 30 percent to the hospitalwide pool, to which is added the savings from the supply utilization program. Specific allocation and distribution of these dollars are described in Chapter 9.

Table 8-2 Summary of Example of Labor Manpower Utilization

Department: MEDICAL NURSING UNIT

Target: 4.05 MH Per Pd   Reward: 4.46 MH Per Pd

	1st Month	2nd Month	3rd Month	Total
Worked hours	5400	5550	5200	16,150
Patient days	1300	1220	1300	3820
Actual level	4.15	4.55	4.00	4.23
Earned hours	5798	5441	5798	17,037
Saved hours	398	(109)	598	996
Average hourly wage index	$ 4.00	$ 4.00	$ 4.00	$ 4.00
Dollars saved	$1592	$(436)	$2392	$3548
Performance Rating (%)	97.6	89.0	101.3	95.7

Chapter 9

Supply Utilization Program

At Baptist Hospital the Supply Utilization Program focuses on the efficient use of material items throughout the institution. This program compares historical usage rates with current rates to determine whether the usage of particular supplies has increased or decreased. When the amount of the change is determined and the cost of the item is known, it is possible to assign a dollar value to the savings (or nonsavings, if this is the case) of the supply.

Design of a program to measure and evaluate utilization of supplies accurately is a complex process. There are many parameters that must be isolated to determine the impact each has on resultant costs. If the unit cost of an item were stable and those factors which create the demand for the item remained constant, effected cost savings for improved utilization of supplies could be determined with an acceptable degree of reliability. This being the case, a simple comparison of the Supply and Expense account for each department from one quarter to the next would indicate the degree of savings associated with any improved utilization. However, this is seldom the case in the health care industry. Another approach had to be considered.

USAGE RATES FOR EACH SUPPLY

One approach that more accurately measures the utilization of supplies involves the development of usage rates for each supply. By the definition used, the usage rate of a supply is the quantity of items consumed in a given period for a definable unit of consumption demand. Demand for supplies increases as numbers of patients and outpatients who utilize the facility increase. Therefore, Baptist needed a unit of consumption demand that combined demand from inpatients and outpatients. Since the philosphy of this hospital is to maintain the same relationship between the cost of providing a service and the charge for that service for both outpatient and inpatient services, total charges for both types of service were used as a common base in creating a meaningful usage rate. The outpatient unit of demand was defined as the equivalent number of patient days which would result in the amount of charges created by outpatient services in a given period of time. To determine the number of outpatient units that occur during a given period, the average charge per inpatient day had to be determined and divided into the total amount of outpatient charges for a given period. The resultant number was the quantity of *outpatient units* for the given period to be added to the number of patient days for the same period to generate the number of *weighted patient units*. This measurement of total demand for supplies became the denominator in the calculation of the usage rates. The numerator in this ratio was the quantity of items issued from the stock, and the resultant usage rate became the key to accurately measuring and evaluating the utilization of supplies.

In management's thinking, the Supply Utilization Program must not only provide a method for determining supply utilization accurately, but it must also provide realistic standards on which sound evaluations of current supply usage can be based. Since there are a number of factors that can significantly affect demand for a supply (technology changes, new products, patient requirements, material shortages, vendor policies), it was decided that a previous twelve-month historical usage rate for each item would be established and adjusted into a standard for each item. It was agreed that a review of these rates should be made each quarter to establish the influencing factors other than improved utilization on usage rates. Because of the difficulty presented by highly fluctuating usages for many new inventory items, the decision was made to consider only those items on inventory for at least twelve months. It should be pointed out that the entire quarter's usage rate for each item was to be compared against the standard usage to minimize the occurrence of nonrepresentative and misleading usage rates that could result because of accounting period cutoffs and departmental ordering habits. The three-month average usage rate then should be more indicative of the true utilization of supplies.

The method of evaluating the savings which results when an improvement has occurred in supply utilization had to be considered with care. There are several ways in which this might be handled. The value of items saved is dependent on the time when these items were purchased. They could be evaluated at the cost of the item when the quarter began, at the cost of the item when the quarter ended, at the average cost of the items in inventory, at the last purchased cost, or any of a number of other costs. Because it was considered to be the most representative of the true cost associated with an item, the average cost of the quantity of each item in inventory was selected. The inventory control system in effect at the hospital generates this average cost statistic for each item in inventory.

The Supply Utilization Program was developed around an existing Materials Management System, which utilizes a computer service provided by a surgical/medical supply organization. With the assistance of their programmer, a program was prepared that automatically maintains the quantities of all stock items issued and computes the usage rates for all items. The computer was further programmed to perform all other calculations required to generate the savings that might be indicated by usage statistics. The concepts on which the supply utilization computer program was based are detailed in this chapter. Similar to the way in which the Manpower Utilization Program compares actual levels against standard levels, the Supply Utilization Program compares actual levels with standard levels. The standards used in this program are developed by considering the previous twelve-month average usage rates for each supply.

HISTORICAL VERSUS STANDARD USAGE RATES

This twelve-month average usage rate has been referred to as the *historical usage rate* and is calculated each quarter for each supply. Initially, the historical usage rate for each supply was determined from the records and adjusted into a *standard usage rate* after careful subjective review. This statistic becomes the standard against which all future usage rates are compared. It should be noted, however, that the historical usage rates are developed each quarter for each supply and can be used to monitor the validity of the initially established standard. If there are obvious reasons why the usage rate of the supply should differ from the preestablished standard, a new standard usage rate can be established.

Both the historical usage rate and the standard usage rate are expressed in terms of units of issue per 1000 weighted patient units. Typical usage rates might appear as 4.0 pounds per 1000 weighted patient units, or 0.023 dozen per 1000 weighted patient units, or 1.20 boxes per 1000 weighted patient units. Note that (1) usage rates were expressed in the same units as the units in which the hospital issues the item, (2) historical usage rates were monthly rates based on averages of twelve-month history, (3) only those items carried in stock for twelve months were considered, and (4) usage rates were all expressed in terms of the base, 1000 weighted patient units. *Weighted patient units* refers to the sum of patient days for inpatient services and the units of outpatient services, which is theoretically equivalent to inpatient days. This was calculated on the basis of census summaries and revenue reports.

Inpatient units = Number of inpatient days

$$\text{Inpatient charges (\$) per patient} = \frac{\text{Inpatient charges (\$)}}{\text{Number of inpatient days}}$$

$$\text{Outpatient units} = \frac{\text{Total outpatient charges (\$)}}{\text{Inpatient charge (\$) per patient day}}$$

Weighted patient units = Number of inpatient units + number of outpatient units

The historical usage rate, therefore, was determined by the following calculation:

$$\text{Historical usage rate} = \frac{\text{Total number of units issued previous twelve months}}{\text{Total weighted patient units previous twelve months}}$$

Standard usage rate = Adjusted historical usage rate

The *current usage rate* was calculated at the end of each item with an established historical usage rate. The current usage rate was calculated in a manner similar to that used for calculating the historical rate, except that only the number of units issued and the weighted patient units for that specific month are considered. The calculation of the current usage rate is as follows:

$$\text{Current usage rate} = \frac{\text{Total number of units issued for current month}}{\text{Weighted sum of patient days and outpatient units for current month}}$$

Another factor needed to calculate supply savings is the *average cost per unit,* the issue value for each unit of a particular stocked item, e.g., $0.025 per dozen or $0.122 per pound. This factor is calculated and routinely maintained by existing inventory programs.

The calculation of supply utilization involves determination of standard cost and actual cost. Since both costs are based on the average cost per unit (as defined above) the effects on inflating supply costs are negligible. *Standard cost* is the cost of using a particular item at the standard usage rate at the current patient load. This cost is calculated by the following formulas:

Standard number units issued = Standard usage rate x Current
1000 patient units

Standard cost = Standard number units issued x Average cost
per unit

Actual cost is calculated similarly, as these formulas illustrate:

Current number units issued = Current usage rate x Current
1000 patient units

Actual cost = Current number units issued x Average cost per
unit

The difference between the standard cost and the actual cost represents dollars saved (or not saved) due to current utilization of supplies. It is important to note that in our Supply Utilization Program, total dollars saved allocated to the Supply Utilization Pool is the net savings for the entire quarter. By using the usage rates for the quarter, sharp fluctuations from month to month (which could justifiably occur) are avoided, and a more realistic indication of true savings is obtained. Similar provision was made for utility factors where variations were within the control of staff.

In the current program, the calculations described are performed by data processing equipment; the summary printout is reviewed each month (Tables 9–1 and 9–2). This review is important because of the possibility that decreases in the usage of particular items in any one month might be due to replacement of those items by other similar ones, or changes in procedure. Review of the printout is intended to verify that dollars saved are savings effected by actual efficiency instead of changes in policy or procedure.

These examples will help you visualize how this method works.

SUPPLY UTILIZATION PROGRAM CALCULATIONS

Suppose that there is a stock supply called Item X, and assume that Item X is issued in dozens.

Previous issue history shows that there have been 380 dozens of Item X issued in the past twelve months. During that same period, there were

Table 9-1 Monthly Supply Usage Report

Item No.	Item Description	Unit Issue	Historical Usage Rate	Current Usage Rate	Average Cost/Unit	Standard Cost	Actual Cost	Dollars Saved
038046	Pen Marks-a-Lot 788	EA	6.19253	1.30841	.473	31.341	6.622	24.719
038049	Paper Carbon Pencil 2 x 4	PK	.23723	.28037	3.358	8.523	10.074	1.551CR
038050	Notebooks Steno 36-746	EA	1.16161	.37383	.485	6.028	1.940	4.088
038051	Paper Pads WHT Ruled 8 1/2x11	EA	6.31524	5.04673	.508	34.327	27.432	6.895
038052	Paper Pads WHT Ruled 8 1/2x14	EA	2.34776	.74766	.542	13.615	4.336	9.279
038053	Thick Lead Pencil W610	EA	4.05746	.74766	.400	17.365	3.200	14.165
038055	Pencils Colored	EA	8.63846	2.24299	.167	15.436	4.008	11.428
038058	Pen Flair Papermate 843/01	EA	8.70390	5.42056	.472	43.958	27.376	16.582
038060	Rubber Bands #3 3 3 1/2In	BX	5.05546	2.89720	.680	36.783	21.080	15.703
038063	Tape Scotch 1/2x1296	EA	4.72007	1.86916	.631	31.868	12.620	19.248
038064	Tape Scotch 3/4x1296	EA	5.27633	2.61682	1.194	67.409	33.432	33.977
038069	Staples Swingline 35	BX	3.49301	1.77570	.950	35.506	18.050	17.456
038072	Paper Carbon 8 1/2 x 11 1/2	BX	.99800	.18692	5.500	58.732	11.000	47.732
038073	Ribbons Typewriter #1010760	BX	.38448	.28037	5.587	22.984	16.761	6.223
038076	Pencil Lead Thick G-920 SCRI	EA	1.86512	1.12150	.250	4.989	3.000	1.989
038079	Paper Gem Clips Jumbo	BX	3.68934	2.42991	.800	31.580	20.800	10.780
038080	Rubber Bands #18 3 In	BX	.44174	.18692	.680	3.214	1.360	1.854
038081	Pencils Mirado #2 1/2	DZ	.13089	.09346	1.800	2.520	1.800	.720
038087	Cards Index Ruled WHT 4x6	IC	15543	.37383	.750	1.247	3.000	1.753CR
038088	Labels Avery S1420 7/8x1 1/4	BX	.06544	.28037	1.620	1.134	4.860	3.726CR
038089	Cards Index WHT Ruled 3x5	IC	6.51975	7.75701	.362	25.253	30.046	4.793CR

250,000 weighted patient units. The historical usage rate is calculated by:

Historical usage rate = 1.52 dozen per 1000 weighted patient units = $\dfrac{380 \text{ dozen issued}}{250,000 \text{ weighted patient units}}$

Standard usage rate = 1.50 dozen per 1000 weighted patient units

Assume that during the past quarter thirty dozen were issued, and there were 25,000 weighted patient units. The current usage rate is calculated as follows:

Current usage rate = 1.20 dozen per 1000 weighted patient units = $\dfrac{30 \text{ Dozen issued}}{250,000 \text{ weighted patient units}}$

It is evident that the hospital has improved its utilization of Item X. In fact, the hospital saved 1.50 minus 1.20, or 0.30 dozen Item X for every 1000 weighted patient units. The number of items actually saved is calculated by comparing standard to actual in the following manner:

1. 1.50 dozen per 1000 weighted patient units x 25,000 weighted patient units = 37.5 dozen standard usage based on current patient load.
2. 1.20 dozen per 1000 weighted patient units x 25,000 weighted patient units = 30.0 dozen actual usage.
3. 37.5 standard –30.0 actual = *7.5 dozen saved.*

To determine dollar savings represented by this 7.5 dozen, management must know the average cost per unit. If the hospital is paying an

Table 9-2 Monthly Supply Usage Report—Summary Sheet

Totals For The Month

Historical Usage Rate	2,308.670
Current Usage Rate	2,126.985
Average Month IP and OP Units	11,113.091
Current Month IP and OP Units	10,700.000
Standard Cost	98,887.370
Actual Cost	92,892.051
Dollars Saved	5,995.319
Employee Portion	2,997.748

average of $30.00 per every dozen of Item X, it follows that by increasing the efficiency of usage of Item X, the department has saved $225.00 (7.5 dozen saved x $30.00 per dozen).

Each quarter, similar calculations are performed for each item in stock, or related items introduced. Total dollars saved, referred to as the Supply Utilization Pool, is combined with the 30 percent factor from the Manpower Utilization Program to form the pool of money that is distributed hospitalwide to all employees. Specific allocation and distribution of these dollars will be described in a later chapter.

Chapter 10

Quality Assurance Program

Experience with incentives at Baptist Hospital over ten years taught us that a measurement of quality is essential for maintenance of professional integrity in a hospital incentive plan. The reworked incentive plan therefore places added emphasis on the factor of quality assurance and incorporates it as a necessary element of the total plan.

A measurement of quality has not been easy for hospitals to acquire! For fifteen years, effort was expended in seeking methods for measuring quality of services rendered by the health care system in general, and by hospitals and the various departments in particular. The methodologies developed in quality measurement efforts typically focused on three approaches:

- Inputs—the availability of adequate and appropriate equipment, facilities, and staff.
- Process—the occurrence of specified activities and measurement of actual performance.
- Outcome—the evaluation of the effectiveness of the process against a desired result.

All three approaches have application in development of quality programs used with an incentive plan. The important consideration is that results of a quality program used with an incentive plan must be departmentally identifiable and oriented to a specific interval of time. Stated another way, a measurement of quality must be defined in such a way as to easily correspond to a *productivity* measurement for labor and supplies.

To satisfy professional concerns, an incentive plan must contain a counterbalancing element that assures that efforts to improve Man-

75

power and Supply Utilization do not result in decreases in quality of service.

Tools to measure quality vary on a wide spectrum from subjective to very objective. They can also vary from simple to complex and sophisticated. The object in selecting the tool for any department should be to select the tool that provides the highest ratio of assessment value versus cost for obtaining the assessment. Numerous hospital areas can be adequately evaluated through completely subjective methods, which are simple and inexpensive. Other departments require more objective methods with higher levels of complexity and sophistication. Accuracy of any assessment is a function of how well the tool measures and evaluates true performance rather than the complexity or sophistication of the tool. Some tools are complex and sophisticated but lack the ability to measure real quality of performance. Conversely, an easy-to-use tool could provide exactly the evaluation required. The same idea applies to use of a subjective tool versus an objective tool. Objectivity is generally better than subjectivity, assuming the proper element is being objectively assessed. However, a sophisticated, highly objective tool that has not been validated through reliability testing might not be providing an assessment of quality as accurately as a purely subjective opinion poll. The point: care must be taken in selecting tools for quality assessment. Quality assurance programs can provide invaluable information for decision making and quality monitoring, but only if thoroughly understood and effectively utilized.

Quality assurance for Baptist Hospital's incentive plan operates through independently developed and maintained programs that vary from highly sophisticated tools to generate unbiased (objective) assessments to extremely subjective tools (such as opinion polls). The level of objectivity and sophistication is established for each department by the hospital's assistant director responsible for that department, based on the ratio of expected value received for the cost incurred. Examples of how departmental quality programs work are given later in the chapter.

QUALITY ASSURANCE OBJECTIVES

Baptist's quality assurance programs were founded on these objectives:

- To assess accurately quality of services being rendered by each hospital department over a given time interval.
- To document areas of activity where improvements in quality are warranted and desirable.

- To provide feedback and permit necessary corrective action.
- To provide a numerical index (if possible) that will accurately identify changes in quality level.

The objective of these programs is to ensure that increasing manpower and supply efficiency or changes in policy or procedures do not cause unacceptable decreases in the level of care quality.

In the revised total incentive plan, all hospital departments can be viewed as a system with three basic components: *inputs* to the system, *processes* of the system, and the *outputs* from the system. In the health care system, inputs include patients; professional, technical, and administrative personnel; facilities, and materials. These inputs process in the system to improve the condition of the patient and produce a completely or partially recovered patient as an output. Quality assurance has traditionally concerned itself with attainment of objectives in the *processing* of the inputs. These objectives are converted into standards against which performance is measured. This type of quality assurance program measures the process of the system and frequently utilizes statistical sampling plans to determine whether the process is "in control;" this traditional approach was chosen as a basis of design and development for most of the departmental quality assurance programs. For departments using this approach, this procedure was typically used:

1. Identification of primary goals and objectives of the department.
2. Identification of factors within a department indicative of the level of achievement for each objective.
3. Definition of minimally acceptable levels for each factor.

With this approach the instruments (or tools) developed became uniquely responsive to the objectives and characteristics of specific departments.

MEASURING TOOLS OF QUALITY ASSURANCE

During initial meetings held with each department head to develop the tool for quality measurement, the department head was asked to identify approximately ten of the department's most pertinent quality attributes. Criteria (and weightings in some cases) were established for each attribute that could be objectively evaluated and measured when audited. Acceptance criteria were specified for each attribute, allowing an observer to assess the condition as "acceptable" or "not acceptable."

Although each measuring tool is unique, the process of administration is typically as follows:

1. The process begins with a periodic inspection of the department's activities to determine the level of achievement for each factor specified, using the tool for that department. The inspector also notes those aspects that are unacceptable.

2. Each factor is rated on degree of acceptability or nonacceptability. Ratings or gradings are recorded and weighted, and the sum of the weighted ratings generates an overall index. (Note: departments frequently weighted all attributes equally.) This index represents a percentage of the total possible score and is referred to as the *Departmental Quality Index*.

3. After results are tabulated a departmental report shows the quality index and illustrates areas of weakness and possible targets for improvements or other actions.

Exhibit 10-1 Sample Department Evaluation

PHARMACY DEPARTMENT
Department Evaluation Report

Date: _____   Time: _____   Auditor: _____

	Designated Area	Acceptable	Not Acceptable*
1. Expiration Dates	Pharmacy		
2. Pricing	"		
3. Narcotic Count	"		
4. Brewer Prepack	"		
5. Credits	"		
6. STAT Orders	Nursing Station		
7. Labels	Pharmacy		
8. Brewer Carts	Nursing Station		
TOTALS			

Quality Rating = $\dfrac{\text{No. Acceptable}}{\text{No. Acceptable + No. Not Acceptable}} \times 100 =$ _____

Comments:
(*Reasons for unacceptable rating (verify with appropriate supervisor))

To maximize benefits from programs of this type, results should be tabulated routinely and reviewed by a quality assurance committee. Responsibility for assimilating and computing quality audit results for quality programs must be centralized in an unbiased administrative person responsible for maintaining an up-to-date Quality Evaluation Manual—one who would aid in training and maintaining rater reliability for all evaluators.

An example of a typical tool used in Quality Assurance is found in the exhibit for Pharmacy (Exhibit 10–1). Here, an evaluation form would be filled out by the evaluator utilizing guidelines for each attribute provided in the Quality Evaluation Manual. For example, the first attribute listed on the evaluation report is "expiration date." The acceptance criterion for this attribute is as follows: "Randomly select ten dated items from the Pharmacy shelves or the refrigerator in the Pharmacy. Reject if the expiration date is exceeded on any of the items."

The evaluator notes on the report that the expiration dates on ten items were acceptable or nonacceptable. Similarly, each attribute is evaluated, and the result recorded on the evaluation sheet. A total is taken on "acceptable" and "not acceptable" responses. Reasons for unacceptable ratings are also indicated on the evaluation sheet. The Quality Rating for this observation is then calculated as follows:

$$\text{Quality rating} = \frac{\text{Number acceptable}}{\text{Number acceptable} + \text{Number not acceptable}} \times 100$$

Several evaluations are made on each department during each quarter. These are accumulated into an overall departmental quality index for the quarter. The quality index then is calculated as follows:

$$\text{Quality index} = \frac{\text{Total number acceptable}}{\text{Total number acceptable} + \text{Total number not acceptable}} \times 100$$

Here's an example of the process. Suppose attributes listed in the chart were rated this way:

	Acceptable	Not Acceptable
1. Expiration Dates	X	
2. Pricing	X	
3. Narcotic Count	X	

	Acceptable (Cont.)	Not Acceptable (Cont)
4. Brewer Prepak		X
5. Credits		X
6. STAT Orders	X	
7. Labels	X	
8. Brewer Carts		X
	5	3

The quality rating for this evaluation would be calculated as follows:

$$\text{Quality rating} = \frac{5}{5+3} \times 100 = 62.5$$

If during the quarter there were eight other evaluations for this department and the total number of acceptable ratings was 49 and the total of not acceptable ratings was 15, the quality index for the quarter would be as follows:

$$\text{Quality index} = \frac{49}{40+15} \times 100 = 76.6$$

The quality index for Pharmacy for this quarter would be 76.6, which could be compared with indices for previous quarters.

THE HOUSEKEEPING EXAMPLE

Development of quality programs for Radiology and Housekeeping was accomplished in the same way as other departmental programs, except that the tools did not resemble those of other departments. In both departments, committees composed of the department head, key employees, and the Medicus staff designed the tools. Both programs were created around a quality factor, which resulted in several check sheets. A brief explanation is given for the Housekeeping program as an example of this approach.

Quality Assurance for Housekeeping evaluates the relative quality level of work performed by Housekeeping personnel. This plan is specifically for Baptist Hospital, Pensacola, developed by representatives of Baptist Hospital, Service-Master Industries, Inc. and Medicus Systems Corporation, using work done by the Executive Housekeepers Advisory Committee for Administrative Service in Hospitals (CASH). It was designed as an administrative tool to improve and maintain improvements made in quality of services rendered by the department.

The Housekeeping Quality Assurance plan samples housekeeping conditions and work situations, evaluating indicators of overall quality, and generating a single periodic departmental quality index.

Six quality assurance evaluation sheets are the principal tools, pinpointing six key areas:

1. Entrance and lobby
2. Patient rooms
3. Housekeeping equipment
4. Corridors, stairwells, and elevators
5. Nurses' stations and utility rooms
6. Departments and administrative areas

Examples of evaluation sheets accompany this section (Exhibits 10–2 and 10–3).

Each evaluation sheet lists factors related to housekeeping functions; each can be scored by direct observation. Maximum score for each factor is indicated on the evaluation sheet. The observer uses his best judgment in rating existing conditions for the factor against the maximum score, which should only be given for absolutely perfect conditions. Factors listed are those considered by housekeeping specialists as key indicators of the quality of service and performance.

The plan requires that twenty observations be made each week with this allocation:

Patient rooms	8 per week
Rest room	2 per week
Lobby and entrance	2 per week
Nurses' station utility	2 per week
Equipment	1 per week
Corridors	2 per week
Stairwells	1 per week
Elevators	1 per week
Departments	1 per week
	20 per week

Day, time, and place for making observations is governed by a random schedule.

Following each control period, the quality index is calculated. This index is proportionate to the percentage of total observations for which an acceptable condition exists. Indices are recorded, posted, and

Exhibit 10-2 Quality Performance Audit

HOUSEKEEPING
Departments & Administrative Offices

Area _____   Room _____

Date _____   Time _____

Factor	Max	Score	Comments
1. Floor clean of dirt, dust, and litter?..........................	5		
2. Floor finished with depth shine? (or carpet clean?).......	10		
3. Waste baskets clean and freshly lined?........................	5		
4. Walls clean and free of spots?....................................	5		
5. Sinks clean?............................	5		
6. Counters clean?......................	5		
7. Ledges free of dust?...............	5		
8. Windows clean?......................	5		
9. Vents clean?...........................	10		
10. Corners clean and neat?........	10		
11. Furniture cleaned and polished?..............................	5		
Total			

Cleanliness Index = _____ ÷ _____ x 100 = _____

Score   Max   Index
Total   Total

Audited By _____

graphed on a performance chart to illustrate trends from period to period. All check sheets are summarized and reviewed each period by Housekeeping supervisory personnel. Corrective action is taken as indicated by information gathered. The performance chart provides a quick

Exhibit 10-3 Quality Performance Audit

HOUSEKEEPING
Patient Rooms

Area ———————————————— Room ————————————————

Date ———————————————— Time ————————————————

Factor	Max	Score	Comments
1. Floor clean of dirt, dust, and litter?...........................	10		
2. Floor finished with depth shine? (or carpet clean?).......	15		
3. Waste basket clean with fresh liner?........................	5		
4. Walls clean and free of spots?.............................	10		
5. Ledges free of dust?..............	10		
6. Windows clean?......................	5		
7. Room orderly?........................	5		
8. Furniture clean?.....................	5		
9. Is toilet bowl clean?..............	10		
10. Odor free?................................	10		
11. Mirror shined?........................	5		
12. Pipes polished?.......................	5		
13. Sink free of soap buildup?....	5		
14. Cubicle curtains, draperies clean?......................................	5		
15. Lights free of dust?...............	5		
16. Blinds clean?...........................	5		
17. Toilet supplies in place?........	5		
18. Vents clean?............................	5		
19. Shower wall free of soap film?..	5		
Total			

Audited By ————————————— Cleanliness Index = ——— ÷ ——— x 100 = ———

graphic picture of trends in housekeeping performance and indicates if significant performance changes have occurred.

Upper and lower control limits can only be developed on the chart after cleanliness indices have stabilized. Several months of inspections are generally required before a process is considered stable and in control. Once this occurs, the mean and the standard deviation of the true population can be estimated, and the resulting upper control limit and lower control limit can be developed. From that point forward, any index points falling outside the quality assurance limits on the chart indicate significant changes in performance level. If the chart indicates a performance change, there is confidence that the change was caused by something other than chance variation (that which is uncontrollable). This would indicate that the true quality level has shifted in the direction indicated. If the chart indicates that there has been a decrease in performance, an assignable cause for the change is sought and corrective action taken.

The Quality Assurance Program for Radiology is similar in design. A major exception is that the factors for Radiology were all given equal weight, where those for Housekeeping have different weights. An example of the Radiology check sheet is given in Exhibit 10–4.

Baptist's Division of Nursing chose to evaluate quality by using a quality monitoring methodology developed jointly by Medicus Systems Corporation and two of its clients, Rush-Presbyterian-St. Luke's Medical Center in Chicago and Baptist Medical Centers in Birmingham, Alabama. Funding for development of the methodology came from the Division of Nursing of the Bureau of Health Resources Development, Department of Health, Education, and Welfare. (A complete report of the study to develop this methodology can be obtained from the Department of Health, Education, and Welfare, Publication Numbers (HRA) 74–25 and (HRA) 76–7.)

Methodology consists of these four elements:

- A comprehensive, explicitly defined structure of the nursing process within which care is evaluated.
- Criteria for evaluation of each segment of the nursing process.
- A set of procedures for use of the criteria.
- A scoring mechanism for translating quality observations into a score for each of the segments of the nursing process defined by the structure.

Structure of the nursing process in this methodology is defined by objectives and subobjectives shown in Exhibit 10–5. Measurement of how

Exhibit 10-4 Service Quality Audit

RADIOLOGY
Special Procedures

Area _____ Date _____
Room _____ Time _____

Factor	Yes	No	Comments
1. Is the policy of no eating and drinking in the x-ray rooms being observed?......			
2. Is sheet clean?..............................			
3. Do surfaces appear free of dust?..........			
4. Are intravenous trays accessible and completely stocked?...............................			
5. Is cabinet well stocked with needed supplies?.................................			
6. Is noise level satisfactory?.....................			
7. Is all equipment in working condition?..............................			
8. Are sinks clean?...................................			
9. Is patient in proper attire and covered?..........................			
10. Is patient getting the immediate attention required?................................			
11. Does patient appear to be comfortable?.......................................			
12. Is conversation discreet?.......................			
13. Has patient received adequate explanation regarding necessary waiting?.......			
14. Has patient received instructions regarding exam procedures?..................			
15. Is patient being assisted on and off x-ray table?..........................			
16. If emergency cart is potentially required, is it nearby and adequately stocked?.................................			
17. Are personnel breaking in proper area?...			

well these factors are met is accomplished through 257 separate criteria applicable to medical, surgical, and pediatric units plus normal newborn nurseries and recovery room. To keep the actual quality monitoring process manageable, not all criteria are used in evaluating the nursing process with regard to any one patient and unit setting. Instead, the master criteria list is divided into subsets from which worksheets are generated. An example of a worksheet is shown in Exhibit 10–6.

Exhibit 10-5 Objective and Subobjective Structure

The Plan of Nursing Care is Formulated
    The condition of the patient is assessed on admission.
    Data relevant to hospital care are ascertained on admission.
    The current condition of the patient is assessed.
    The written plan of nursing care is formulated.
    The plan of nursing care is coordinated with the medical plan of care.

The Physical Needs of the Patient are Attended
    The patient is protected from accident and injury.
    The need for physical comfort and rest is attended.
    The need for physical hygiene is attended.
    The need for a supply of oxygen is attended.
    The need for activity is attended.
    The need for nutrition and fluid balance is attended.
    The need for elimination is attended.
    The need for skin care is attended.
    The patient is protected from infection.

The Nonphysical (Psychological, Emotional, Mental, Social) Needs of the Patient are Attended
    The patient is oriented to hospital facilities on admission.
    The patient is extended social courtesy by the nursing staff.
    The patient's privacy and civil rights are honored.
    The need for psychological-emotional well-being is attended.
    The patient is taught measures of health maintenance and illness prevention.
    The patient's family is included in the nursing care process.

Achievement of Nursing Care Objectives is Evaluated
    Records document the care provided for the patient.
    The patient's response to therapy is evaluated.

Unit Procedures are Followed for the Protection of All Patients
    Isolation and decontamination procedures are followed.
    The unit is prepared for emergency situations.

The Delivery of Nursing Care is Facilitated by Administrative and Managerial Services.
    Nursing reporting follows prescribed standards.
    Nursing management is provided.
    Clerical services are provided.
    Environmental and support services are provided.

Quality in any nursing unit is monitored through review of 10 percent of one months' patient census. Observations are distributed randomly across days and times of day (except that no observations are taken on the night shift). A master schedule defined for nurse observers states the number of observations to be made by shift on each unit. Patients are randomly selected from the unit prior to actual observations. Once patients have been identified for observation, their illness classifications are ascertained and worksheets are selected. A general unit observation is made at the same time.

At month's end, a computer program produces indices for the twenty-eight subobjectives. The "score" indicated for each subobjective is the average of the criteria scores within the subobjective. All criteria within a subobjective are treated equally, with no attempt made to weight relative importance of the particular attribute of nursing addressed by the subobjective. Indices for major objectives are computed as average values of the subobjective scores within a given objective. A sample quality report is shown as Exhibit 10–7.

Other more subjective programs are used at Baptist for Dietary, the Gift Shop, the Chaplaincy Department, Admitting, and the Patient Representatives. Tools such as Patient Opinion Polls (mailed to the patient at home after his hospital stay or taken while the patient is still in the hospital) help evaluate these departments. The opinion polls questionnaire is shown as Exhibit 10–8. Additional programs that provide valuable input include routine physician polls, communitywide telephone polls, and periodic special employee surveys.

Exhibit 10-6

IN A PLAN OF CARE IS THERE A STATEMENT ABOUT ACTIVITIES THE PATIENT IS EXPECTED TO DO FOR HIMSELF AND ACTIVITIES THE NURSING STAFF SHOULD PERFORM FOR THE PATIENT?

No — 1
Yes — 2

Check lists acceptable: Refers to all ADL, e.g. eating, toilet, dressing, bathing, walking, etc. and other types of participation in care (wound dressing, etc.)

ARE MEDICALLY PRESCRIBED TREATMENTS INCLUDED IN THE NURSING CARE RECORDS?

No — 1
Yes—incomplete — 2
Yes—complete — 3
Not applicable — 4

Check nursing record of treatments with current medical orders for this patient.

IS THERE A NURSING PLAN FOR MAKING OBSERVATIONS OF SIGNS OR SYMPTOMS IN REGARD TO MEDICAL TREATMENT, MEDICATIONS, DISEASE PROCESS OR POSSIBLE COMPLICATIONS?

No — 1
Yes — 2
Not applicable — 3

Refers to major signs and symptoms in regard to this patient's present condition. Does not apply to observations indicated in physician's orders. Observer must determine if patient condition indicates need for specific observation.

Code yes if any level nursing plan exists.

IS BOWEL FUNCTION RECORDED DAILY?

No — 1
Yes — 2

Narrative or graphic records are acceptable. Review for previous 5 days; if patient on unit less than 5 days, review for length of time patient on unit.

IS THERE A WRITTEN STATEMENT IN REGARD TO THE FAMILY'S LEVEL OF UNDERSTANDING OF THE PATIENT'S CONDITION?

No — 1
Yes, name of diagnosis, surgery or test — 2
Yes, understanding of illness stated — 3
Not applicable — 4

Refers to any time during hospitalization. Refers to responses probably elicited by question: "CAN YOU TELL ME SOMETHING ABOUT MR. ___'S CONDITION?" "Level of understanding" defined in answer codes.

DO RECORDS DOCUMENT THE REASONS FOR OMISSION OF MEDICATIONS?

No — 1
Yes, some of the time — 2
Yes, most of the time — 3
Yes, all of the time — 4
Not applicable — 5

Refers to past 7 days: If patient on unit less than 7 days, consider whatever time patient has been on this unit.

Exhibit 10-7 Nursing Quality Report

June-July 1974 Units

	A	B	C	D	E	F	G	H
Condition Is Assessed On Admission	59	78	43	78	85	62	64	73
Data Relevant To Care Is Ascertained	43	73	43	64	86	63	61	62
Current Condition Is Assessed	30	42	16 *	38	28	46	50 *	41
The Written Plan Is Formulated	65	48	34	53	40	31	49	25
Plan Is Coordinated With Medical Plan	82	58	55	79	66	78	54	33
Care Plan Formulated								
	55	59	38	62	61	56	55	46
Patient Is Protected From Accident And Injury	95	97	98	96	83	90	93	100
Need For Comfort & Rest Is Attended	96	79	88	97	79	70	80	70
Need For Phys. Hygiene Is Attended	95	87	83	93	91	80	66	76
Need For Supply Of Oxygen Is Attended	100 *	100 *	100 *	100	87	100	100 *	
Need For Activity Is Attended	44	79	83 *	96	100 *	66 *	78 *	41
Need For Nutrients & Fluid Balance Is Attended	83	89	98	100	71	68	69	100 *
Need For Elimination Is Attended	88	87 *	66	71	100	41 *	66	100
Need For Skin Care Is Attended	64	37	75	0 *	50	88	50	100 *
Patient Is Protected From Infection	79	75	96	70	81	100	95	100 *
Physical Needs Attended								
	82	81	87	80	82	78	77	85
Patient Is Oriented To Hospital Facility On Admission	57	66	74	67	60	46	61	64
Patient Is Extended Courtesy By Staff	98	71	96	85	98	77	76	94
Patient Privacy & Rights Are Honored	83	82	82	76	66	75	71	85
Psycho-emotional Well-being Is Attended	61	77	54	61	78	57	65	67
Patient Taught Health Maintenance & Illness Prevention	88	62	64	43	67	62	61	68
Patient's Family Is Included In Care Process	62	37	40	66	60	41	50	48
Non-physical Needs Attended								
	74	65	68	66	71	59	64	71
Records Document Care Provided	65	63	46	60	42	70	47	47
Patient Response To Therapy Is Evaluated	46	23	36	41	25	33	27	46
	55	43	41	50	33	51	37	46
Isolation And Decontamination Procedures Are Followed	95	91	50	93	100	48	72	100
Unit Is Prepared For Emergency Situation	96	99	99	92	82	100	77	87
Unit Procedures Followed								
	95	95	74	92	91	74	74	93
Nurse's Report Follows Prescribed Standards	87	85	84	87	82	87	85	83
Nursing Management Is Provided	85	83	82	72	89	83	91	83
Clerical Services Are Provided	86	75	83	93	85	88	89	82
Environmental & Support Services Are Provided	85	60	70	75	69	57	79	68
Delivery Of Care Facilitated								
	85	75	79	81	81	78	86	79

Blank Score -	Indicates No Valid Responses
*	Indicates Insufficient Valid Responses For Reliable Score

Exhibit 10-8 Patient Opinion Poll

(Please Check One)

ADMITTING OFFICE   Excellent Good Average Poor

a. Courtesy   ☐ ☐ ☐
b. Promptness   ☐ ☐ ☐
c. Pre-admitted   ☐ ☐ ☐

COMMENTS _____

ROOM ACCOMMODATIONS

a. Room Clean   ☐ ☐ ☐
b. Comfort   ☐ ☐ ☐
c. Quietness   ☐ ☐ ☐

COMMENTS _____

NURSING STAFF

a. Courteous   ☐ ☐ ☐ ☐
b. Efficient   ☐ ☐ ☐ ☐
c. Prompt   ☐ ☐ ☐ ☐
d. Concern   ☐ ☐ ☐ ☐

COMMENTS _____

(Please Check One)

Excellent Good Average Poor

FOOD SERVICES

a. Appetizing   ☐ ☐ ☐
b. Proper temperature   ☐ ☐ ☐
c. Sufficient   ☐ ☐ ☐

COMMENTS _____

SERVICES FROM OTHER HOSPITAL PERSONNEL

a. Laboratory   ☐ ☐ ☐
b. X-ray   ☐ ☐ ☐
c. Dietary   ☐ ☐ ☐
d. Housekeeping   ☐ ☐ ☐
e. Volunteer   ☐ ☐ ☐
f. Therapist   ☐ ☐ ☐
g. Pastoral Care   ☐ ☐ ☐
h. Patient Representatives   ☐ ☐ ☐
Other _____   ☐ ☐ ☐

BUSINESS OFFICE

a. Courtesy   ☐ ☐ ☐
b. Promptness   ☐ ☐ ☐
c. Explanation   ☐ ☐ ☐

COMMENTS _____

GENERAL

A. Have you been a patient here before?
Yes ____ No ____

B. How did this stay compare to your previous stay?
Better ____
Equal ____
Not as Good ____

C. Have you been hospitalized elsewhere?
Yes ____ No ____

D. If so, how did your stay here compare to your stay in another hospital?
Better ____
Equal ____
Not as Good ____

In general, was the care you received

Excellent   Good   Average   Poor

We'd like to know your general impression of us.

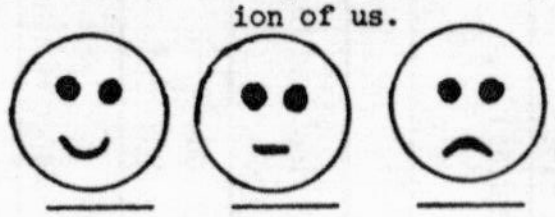

☺   😐   ☹   (Please Check One)

COMMENTS OR SUGGESTIONS.

_____

Should you like to talk to us directly, please call Patient Relations at 555-1234.

Chapter 11

The Total Plan

Effectiveness of these programs, and therefore the effectiveness of the plan itself, depended on several factors:

1. Incorporation of the utilization programs and the department quality monitoring programs into a well-defined, appropriately balanced incentive package.
2. Employee awareness of policies and procedures of the plan.
3. Establishment of areas of responsibility for administration and maintenance of the plan.

These programs have been incorporated into the total incentive plan. The Manpower Utilization Program and the Supply Utilization Program encourage improved utilization of resources; the Quality Assurance Programs monitor quality of work performance. But there is a cardinal point: engineers and management recognize that it is important to hospital, patient, and employees that efficiency be improved and maintained; it is of even greater importance that quality of patient care not be jeopardized by efficiencies. Use of employee incentive plans in industry has resulted in efficiency increases and quality improvements. The goal in the hospital is to ensure that as efficiency is improved, quality is maintained.

INCENTIVE REWARD CHECKS

Each quarter, the Department of Administrative Services (which is responsible for the plan) calculates monies to be allocated to departmental and combined pools of dollars saved. Total dollars saved are divided equally between the employees and the patients. Patients receive their share through lower hospitalization costs, improved methods of care, better facilities and equipment. Employee share comes via quarterly incentive reward checks.

The total of employee checks is dependent on the dollar amount of funds to be distributed and the hours worked by the employee during the quarter. There are two limiting factors on dollars distributed in any quarter: first, the hospital must have funds available to pay incentive reward checks. If the hospital is unable in any quarter to pay the checks, the amount not paid is carried over and paid with the following quarter's incentive checks. The second restriction is that the total dollars distributed shall not exceed an established ceiling that reflects an optimally desirable level of productivity and is established relative to employee wage rates. Baptist Hospital's belief is that the incentive plan should not be out of phase with individual earnings; individual rewards would not exceed 15 percent of normal earnings.

One aspect of the revised plan that differs from the original incentive program is the policy of eligibility. Generally, all employees who have successfully completed their probationary period (generally ninety days) are eligible to receive incentive reward checks. One additional requirement is that a recipient must be employed at the time incentive reward checks for the quarter are distributed (the only exception is for retirees). These requirements for participation encourage incoming employees to become oriented to jobs more rapidly and become effective performers. The requirement, coupled with the repetitive nature of the plan, encourages personnel to remain active participants in the delivery of quality care.

An example of the calculation and distribution of incentive payments is shown in Table 11–1.

Table 11-1 Manpower Utilization Program

Department	Target Level	Reward Level	Hours Worked	Workload	Earned Hours	Saved Hours	$ Per Manhour	Dollars Saved	Departmental Portion	Hospitalwide Portion
Maintenance	11.75	12.93	13,423	1,100	14,223	800	4.15	3,320	1,162	498
Housekeeping	30.45	33.50	33,575	1,050	35,175	1600	2.65	4,240	1,484	636
Laundry	1.61	1.71	9,556	5,025	8,593	0	2.96	0	0	0
Grand Total			513,638		472,411	10,500		36,000	12,600	5,400

Supply Utilization Program
    Total Dollars Saved..$6,000
    Employee Portion (Hospitalwide)................................. 3,000
    Total Hospitalwide Pool........................$5,400 + $3,000 = $8,400

DISTRIBUTION

Since the amount of incentive payment paid to each employee is determined by department, the calculation for a Housekeeping Department employee will be shown in this example:

Number of Housekeeping Employees	65
Total Number of Hospital Employees	1,000
Housekeeping Employee Incentive Payment:	
Housekeeping Portion 1484/65	= $22.83
Hospitalwide Portion 5400/1000	= 8.40
Total Incentive Payment, Housekeeping	$31.23

The remaining determination of the incentive payment amount is the departmental quality index. The index for Housekeeping in the example period was 83.5, above the minimum acceptable level of 75.0 for that department. If the quality index had been below the acceptable level, the assistant director with authority over the department would have had the right to cancel all or part of the department's incentive pay.

Calculation and distribution of incentive rewards is the key to Manpower and Supply Utilization Programs; however, of equal importance is continuing feedback through reporting to each department the progress made toward better efficiencies accrued during each calendar period. Each month, in addition to calculating dollar savings, the Department of Administrative Services computes performance ratings for each department. Reports compiled for each department and the hospital as a whole are distributed to supervisory personnel for review and sharing with the staff.

During each quarter, as audits are performed, results of quality indices and the narratives on quality of performance are compiled into reports distributed to supervisory personnel. At the end of the quarter, departments receive performance reports summarizing quarterly efficiency and quality for the past twelve months, generating constructive effort toward improved performance.

EMPLOYEE AWARENESS PROGRAM

No employee can be expected to perform effectively if he is unaware of what is required of him, how he can best satisfy those requirements, and the degree of his progress toward improvements. The Employee Awareness Program was designed as a supportive element of the incentive plan and to provide adequate communications.

This program does not have detailed procedures. The Employee Awareness Program is merely the name applied to the collective efforts given to administration, administrative services, and supervisory personnel to make the incentive plan a meaningful part of each employee's day. The specific activities that this program incorporates are determined by management on the basis of the goals we wish to achieve. In general, Baptist's management believes these goals should be:

1. To acquaint the employee as fully as possible with the details of the program relating to its design, its characteristics, it objectives, and all policies and procedures.
2. To demonstrate to the employee how his personal goals can be more fully satisfied by striving to achieve the goals of the hospital.
3. To create an atmosphere in the hospital and an attitude among employees conducive to attainment of cost control and quality of care —one that affords high visibility to the incentive plan on a daily basis.
4. To make distribution of incentive reward checks and performance reports a special affair, something eagerly anticipated.
5. To make the employees aware not only of how well they may have performed but also of where they have fallen short and how they might improve performance.

There are a number of mechanisms for employee awareness. Hospital publications, continuing education programs, and bulletin boards are primary media. Work improvement seminars can be effective for illustrating to the employee the specific measures he can take to increase his incentive reward check. Employee suggestion plans offer the mechanism for implementation of major money-saving ideas by providing special individual recognition and financial rewards. Dinners, picnics, special incentive reward check days provide the needed atmosphere for participation in the plan. In all of these, management seeks an atmosphere that makes the wasteful employee feel "out of touch" with his peers.

In over a decade, Baptist Hospital has learned that the success of an incentive plan is related to the direction, intensity, and quality of the efforts expended to support it. Support includes initial and ongoing activities involved with conveying philosophy, concepts, and procedures to employees; definition of areas of responsibility for administration and maintenance of the plan; and continuing efforts toward ensuring that the plan is enthusiastically and properly managed and supported.

Tactical responsibilities for administration and maintenance of the Employee Productivity Incentive Plan are currently in the Department of Administrative Services. Duties of this department, with respect to this plan, include specification of policies and procedures (subject to administration approval); collection of all data; calculation of incentive rewards; compilation of various performance reports for efficiency and quality; maintenance and improvement of all aspects of the total plan, including standards, quality tools, and general procedures; and general technical support of any activities directly related to the plan management. At Baptist Hospital, this function reports directly to administration and has no general line authority, other than that specifically delegated by administration.

SUPPORT CANNOT BE OVEREMPHASIZED

By now this latter point might have been overemphasized, but it bears repeating once more. This incentive plan depends largely on the support given it by division heads, department heads, and supervisory personnel. These people are responsible for creating proper attitudes; use of the incentive philosophy with their own management techniques creates the necessary daily emphasis on cost-consciousness and quality. To develop a usable record, management personnel must provide input to the Department of Administrative Services on a continuing basis, input that includes not only data necessary for efficiency and quality calculations but also relevant input on policy and procedural changes within their areas of responsibility. All supervisory personnel have the potential for making or breaking the plan; and the importance of their support, not only in adhering to specified policies and procedures but also in enthusiastically supporting the philosophies of the plan, cannot be stressed enough.

Administrative personnel have an interest and a responsibility of the highest order related to the incentive plan. They are to ensure that the plan goals are consistent with hospital objectives and that policies of the plan are equitable and consistent with the welfare of the employees. The plan must be recognized as a meaningful long term program, not a stopgap measure or management gimmick. The administration must make a meaningful commitment to providing philosophical and material support to the plan, and this support must be of such a magnitude as to create enthusiasm on a day-to-day versus a one-day-a-quarter basis. With proper support and judicious application of the incentive concepts incorporated in the Employee Incentive Plan, hospital management will greatly enhance its efforts in the achievement of hospital goals.

That is the way management and those who structure it view this method. Looking back over this hospital's history of work with incentives, most people involved believe they have found a tool that benefits everyone. It is not necessarily an easy tool to use— but then, what is?

Chapter 12

In Retrospect—Some Don'ts!

Now that Baptist Hospital has embarked on a new version of its program, there have been opportunities to reflect on the lessons of a decade. Those reflections include numerous discussions with persons in other hospitals who attempted our methods, or others designed to reach a similar goal. Since everyone profits from the mistakes of others, those who collaborated on this book felt that it would be wise at this point—hoping that the reader *is* giving thought to making an attempt himself—to illustrate some of the pitfalls we discovered. As in other sections, this chapter suggests that all hospitals are unique; no single method or roadblock applies uniformly to all.

There are a great many principles that might be considered; I have chosen just five pitfall points because they were items either prominent in Baptist's program or ones others felt were critical.

YOU'VE GOT TO BE A BELIEVER

This is fundamental to everything else. Productivity incentives are not some sort of game; they are part of management tactics, such as public relations or benefit programs. Incentives are also part of a person's own economic philosophy; either he believes in incentives *in hospitals* or he does not. Over the years, I have found a large number of people who still do not believe that incentives will work in hospitals. They feel the tactic is foreign to the hospital environment; or, if they see that the plan works in our hospital, they still doubt its applicability to theirs. Or, they can see possibilities in *some* departments, but not in others, usually because of some strong personalities who might stand in opposition. If any or all of these question marks are present, my advice is: STOP! Like most other attempts, this program will succeed only if the people at the top are believers! They have got to be convinced that what they are proposing is good, and right, and workable. There must be a personal commitment backed up with enough energy and willpower to see it through.

Recently a new book appeared about the Wright Brothers, reviewing the frustrations Wilbur Wright suffered as he tried to get into the air. His story illustrates my point very well. He painstakingly observed nature; he studied his observations; he used trial and error, practical experimentation, basic research—employing all of the tools available at the time. When he had achieved basic flight and *knew* his principles were sound, he polished and confirmed his findings.

Incentives are similar. They represent a risk; but they also offer great rewards of a type we need in our hospitals. To make an incentive program fly, you must be a believer!

PRODUCTIVITY INCENTIVES ARE NO SUBSTITUTE FOR GOOD SUPERVISION

In the late 1960s, as John Schill, John Appleyard, and I began holding seminars to explain the incentives plan, there were several hospital people who quickly envisioned incentives as a substitute for supervision. They reasoned:

> "By having the financial carrot in front of people, they'll work better and overcome the built-in problems that some supervisors cannot seem to control. Incentives will help prevent absenteeism, tardinesss, scheduling arguments, and the like. Instead of fighting the problem of weak supervision, we'll install incentives!" They could not have been more wrong.

After viewing what happened at Baptist Hospital, I'd put it this way:

> *"Incentives will make good supervisors better, but they are not a crutch and certainly will not replace the application of sound supervisory actions."*

Permit this example. Baptist had one department where it enjoyed what I would call good, basic supervision and where the staff introduced one of the least complicated formulas. The only serious ongoing problem in that department was communications, which were not the supervisor's strong point. What happened? The incentive program sputtered badly because the supervisor, continuing her obvious shortcoming, failed to conduct monthly meetings to distribute incentive checks and explain results. Instead of introducing a program that helped correct a problem, the management compounded one. People grew restive and frustrated because they did not understand incentive results. It took hard work—and some straightforward supervisory counseling—to get things right. Ultimately, both situations were corrected; thus, I guess one could say the incentive program did a double-barreled job for the hospital.

I would have to urge any administrator to discard thoughts that an incentive will *per se* solve problems of weakness in his staff. Weak supervisors generally will be ineffective in using incentive tools as motivators. If you are running a ship with a weak crew, do not count on incentives to bail the boat. It will not work. Peter Drucker commonly repeats a phrase in his books: "Build upon strengths!" That's true in this program. If the staff is not strong, delay incentives until it is.

YOUR PEOPLE HAVE TO HAVE FAITH IN YOU

Back in 1964 when we first contemplated our plan and John Schill was making his initial observations in our Laundry, the two of us talked a lot about how to begin. After all, the beginning had to be with shallow data; there were no hospital precedents. John and I knew we were going to make errors and would have to make many corrections in the ground rules. John put the thing pretty well when he said: "If people trust us and have faith, it'll work. If not, the whole thing's not worth fooling with."

He was so right! A plan of this kind must operate on a base of mutual trust. The hospital leadership has got to be able to tell its story to people in department after department and know that what they say will fall on receptive ears. There *must* be a track record that illustrates mutual trust. Without this, the plan has little hope. Incentives require a team operation. They help blend men and women into a working force through which they and others will benefit. On the surface, explaining such a concept seems easy; after all, you're saying "... if you work smarter, you'll make more money." There are few better ways to get someone's attention. But if there is a serious possibility that dissidents are present who would willingly embarrass the administration and the hospital, beware! The old Latin phrase "caveat emptor" is usually applied to the marketplace. But I think it applies here, too. Before you, as an executive, "buy" incentives, beware: be sure the people have enough faith in *you* to help make the plan work. If that faith is lacking, then you have some other homework to do.

PRODUCTIVITY INCENTIVES ARE FOR THE COST CONSCIOUS

A lot has been said about cost consciousness in earlier chapters, but the point bears repeating. Many of today's hospitals have been operated without the kind of cost consciousness that identifies successful private business. That is not an indictment of administration; it is a reflection on the time, in which so often government policy has encouraged hospitals to be inefficient.

The picture *is* changing; that is why I believe incentives are moving into a rosier spotlight. But before your hospital takes the critical first step, be sure your total management staff knows it must concentrate on cost control. Make sure they know your consideration of this program is not some kind of smokescreen. Americans have gone through a generation in which many areas of health care have had a "cost-plus" philosophy; it has been a time in which the total objective was "more and bigger," with little concern for what it cost.

Incentives require a totally different attitude. If your staff is not oriented to those terms, STOP! No group can make incentives a motivational factor without cost control as basic policy.

DO NOT TRY TO BUILD ROME IN A DAY

When I was a boy, my Latin teacher used to try to slow fast-moving students by reminding them it took the Romans quite a while to build their empire. Incentives is one area where patience and careful building are virtues.

It is not easy for a hospital to install incentives in all areas simultaneously; in most cases, it required months to make an orderly introduction of plans, beginning with those departments where implementation was easiest and had the greatest possibility of success.

As this book has suggested, Baptist Hospital moved a step at a time; there was soon pressure to act with greater dispatch, but management declined. The new method ultimately developed by the Medicus men, Jim Hicks and Ernest Williamson, enables hospitals to move more quickly, even across the total institution simultaneously. There is no road map that will guide you with certainty, for circumstances vary with each hospital. Our hospital began in the Laundry because there were reasons to do so; others have found Housekeeping or Dietary more receptive initial targets. The main consideration is to find a place where there is a real chance for success.

THE FIRST STEP MUST BE SURE

There are other pitfalls, I'm sure, but these five areas are to me the most significant. At the outset, *you* must be a believer; the team is led from the top, and that's where the firmest commitment must be made. Incentives are a motivator, not a replacement for good supervision. To install such a program, those who will work with it must have faith in the institution and in the people who direct it. Incentives are for those who are truly cost conscious. Also, the process must be installed in an orderly progression so step by step it can be assimilated into the overall operation.

Perhaps all this can be summed up in a statement attributed to Charlie Grimm, who managed on and off in the major leagues for many years. "Jolly Chollie" supposedly put it this way: "A manager usually tries to get a three-year contract. Except in unusual circumstances, he's been hired because the team's been going badly. He knows he'll need one year to put his house in order, one year to build, and hopefully he'll make a good showing in that third year and save his bacon."

His philosophy can help us. We need one year to clean our houses and get things ready; we need a year to rebuild in the new image; and by that third year, things should begin to pay off. Incentives are like that.

To judge the success of Baptist Hospital's incentive program, the interested reader will want to examine the following tables, which illustrate the effect on costs of these programs. The tables examine the hospital's operating data for the period 1963–74, a comparison of the hospital cost per patient day with other hospitals of similar character in Florida and the United States, similar data on cost per admission, an analysis of payroll as a percent of total expense, a comparison of average annual salaries, other expenses per patient day, some general observations, and then some basic analyses of departmental productivity, which help illustrate the effect of this type of program on the output of employees. In the comparison with other hospitals, data are taken from the official AHA Guide Issues.

Appendices

Appendices

Appendix A

Reports of Four Independent Studies

J. J. JEHRING REPORT—JANUARY 1968

The Use of Subsystem Incentives in Hospitals: A Case Study of the Incentive Program at Baptist Hospital, Pensacola, Florida

In 1968, J. J. Jehring, late director of the Center for the Study of Productivity Motivation, The University of Wisconsin, conducted studies of the subsystem incentive system at Baptist Hospital. The purpose of Jehring's study was to prepare a report describing new incentive approaches capable of raising employee productivity and reducing costs in the nonprofit hospital. The report represented two weeks of intensive investigation into aspects of operation of incentive programs at Baptist, ranging from an analysis of data concerning performance of individual departments to the entire hospital to an attitude survey of employees and interviews with most key management personnel. Conclusions of the study were reported in the report entitled, *The Use of Subsystem Incentives in Hospitals: A Case Study of the Incentive Program at Baptist Hospital, Pensacola, Florida* as follows:

1. It is possible to design subsystem incentives for hospitals that will result in increased productivity.
2. Using subsystem incentives it is possible to raise wages without raising costs.
3. Subsystem incentives are easier to apply in some departments than in others.
4. Nursing departments pose special problems in applying subsystem incentive plans.

5. Subsystem incentive programs tend to make hospital employees more receptive to methods improvements.

6. It is difficult and takes experimentation to design departmental formulas that will give comparable rewards for comparable performance to individuals in the different departments. As more experience is obtained in a variety of hospitals, this may be solved.

7. Subsystem formulas should be designed to meet the special needs of each hospital.

8. Too great a difference in productivity shares paid between departments can result in poor interdepartmental cooperation.

9. Little incentive will result from a total systems incentive (such as the Baptist Incentive Retirement Trust) unless a definite program is instituted which makes effective use of the motivational potentials in the plan.

To be most effective, subsystem incentive programs must be accompanied by good management practices. The program of subsystem incentives used at Baptist Hospital has proved a successful experiment in designing and operating a financial incentive for a nonprofit community hospital. Through it a number of the cost-saving goals established by the administration for various departments were achieved.

Subsystem incentive plans as they relate to hospitals generally give rise to a number of problems, and as a result they require more experimentation and research on a broader basis to make them fully useful to the health industry in the U.S.

AMERICAN HOSPITAL ASSOCIATION REPORT—APRIL 1969

Innovative Hospital Management Programs: A Summary of Ten Case Studies

In 1969, the American Hospital Association and The Department of Health, Education, and Welfare jointly sponsored a comprehensive three-month pilot study of innovative management programs that had been implemented to achieve economy. HEW's interest was a result of their need for assistance with the development of incentive reimbursement programs. The AHA formed two multidisciplinary teams of five members each; each team included a certified public accountant, an industrial engineer, a behavioral scientist, a physician, and a hospital administrator to analyze current innovative programs in hospitals throughout the United States. The goal was to judge the effect on cost reduction or containment and whether the programs adversely affected quality of care. The Productivity Incentive Program at Baptist was one of ten care programs evaluated. Conclusions reached by the evaluation team on this program were as follows:

1. "The quality of care at Baptist Hospital is likely to have been enhanced by management innovation ... although not all members of the hospital's medical staff favor the productivity incentive program," reported the physician team member.
2. "The plan has the approval of these (Baptist Hospital) employees and has made them extremely cost conscious," reported the teams' certified public accountant.
3. "The program has in no way been harmful to job satisfaction and in terms of reducing absenteeism, has been helpful," reported the team's behavioral scientist.
4. The program "has led to greater personal involvement of personnel and that this, in turn, has led to improved job performance," the team concluded.

ABT ASSOCIATES REPORT—DECEMBER 1973

Productivity-Incentive Program in Baptist Hospital

Hospitals in the United States in 1973 were under pressure to at least contain, if not reduce, spiraling hospital costs. Hospital officials had been trying since the Economic Stabilization Program's Phase I introduction in 1971 to determine ways in which costs could be contained. Several studies were commissioned by the Department of Health, Education, and Welfare and other federal agencies to identify potential methods. One study was conducted by Abt Associates, Inc., of Cambridge, Massachusetts, a consulting firm. Their in-depth analysis on Baptist Hospital's program consolidated recently proposed changes into their report. Report of this analysis was published in December 1973. Although it did not depict the method of calculating incentive checks for the hospital at that time, the report was comprehensive and was considered by the hospital as a synthesis of the existing program and the program they wanted to develop. The formulas included a manhour factor, a supply factor, a quality factor, and the patient opinion index. Manhours worked were used in the formulas, and each department had a standard manhours established per procedure or workload volume. Quality was discussed as a factor to be used in a final adjustment of the payout.

Abt reported that there were clear indications that the productivity incentive program at Baptist had "some impact on employee efficiency." The report added that there was "a general slipping in its productivity" in recent years when there had been less emphasis on the program (because of IRS's position). On the program's impact on patient care, the report said that "the author could find no evidence of a general improvement or slipping in the quality of patient care. In those areas where quality control programs have been established, there is no evidence of a decline in quality ... in most quality has improved based on these indicators." On the program's impact on costs, the report states that Baptist "was able to keep its per diem costs in check while the national and state averages soared."

LITTLEJOHN REPORT—MAY 1975

Review and Analysis of Employee Incentives in Health Care Institutions

In 1975, Roy Littlejohn Associates, Inc., entered into contract with the Bureau of Health Services Research, Department of Health, Education, and Welfare, to conduct a study entitled *Review and Analysis of Employee Incentives in Health Care Institutions*. The purpose of the study was to identify, describe, and document the state-of-the-art of employee incentive plans in use in hospitals and assess their relative effectiveness in increasing productivity. In the interim report published in May 1975, these comments were made regarding the Baptist program:

1. We conclude that material, both published and unpublished, describing and analyzing the incentive plans used by Long Beach Memorial Hospital, Long Beach, California, and Baptist Hospital, Pensacola, Florida ... essentially represent the state-of-the-art so far as monetary employee incentive plans in short-term hospitals are concerned.
2. Employee incentive plans used with other personnel motivation systems and good management practices will aid in increasing employee productivity and reducing or containing costs.
3. The general conclusion of the Littlejohn Report concerning the reviewed literature was as follows:

With two notable exceptions (Baptist and Long Beach), employee incentive plans in hospitals seem to experience a short life. The reviewed literature, as well as the documentation seems to indicate this is basically because employee incentive plans are generally designed for a given set of unstable conditions, such as cost factors, limitations in physical facilities and problems with employee behavior. When these conditions are altered, or the hospital expands its facilities or changes its organization, management seems disinclined to update and adjust the incentive plan to meet the new conditions. Employee incentive plans are perhaps the most difficult of the various innovative management techniques to implement, but because of the labor intensive characteristic of the hospital industry they may also be potentially the most rewarding. Undoubtedly, the management knowledge and information acquired necessarily through the operation of an employee incentive plan will improve the ability of hospital administrators to predict, plan and operate the hospital's overall medical service program. The reviewed literature does disclose that if the following five conditions are generally met, the incentive plan's changes for success are markedly increased:

1. The standard employee performance indices are based on a current professional (industrial engineer) analysis of inputs (labor and materials) that will produce a standard output (product) under normal conditions. The standard should not be based exclusively on past historical performance, though this data may be of considerable value in proofing the final standard performance determination.
2. All hospital departments and personnel have an opportunity to participate in the employee incentive plan.
3. Incentive payments are paid to the employees when they are earned, preferably by a separate check designated as incentive payment.
4. The incentive program is regularly supervised, and must be repeatedly explained and promoted to participating employees.
5. Incentive productivity payments are not the sole employee reward available, and the incentive plan is complementary to other good management and personnel motivation and recognition systems.

An imperative prerequisite to the installation of any type of incentive plan is an organizational atmosphere of good labor-management relations and sound supervisory and personnel practices. The success of an employee incentive plan is directly related to how well management fulfills both the employee's human and financial needs.

Available literature and our independent field investigation point to the hospitalwide, cost sharing-type employee incentive plan, as being the most effective (type of plan) as an aid to hospitals in their efforts to increase employee productivity and contain rising hospitalization costs.*

---

*Baptist Hospital's program is an exception. Here officials believe that the closer the proximity of employees to the source of the action, the greater their interest and ability to contribute to efficiency.

Appendix B

Before and After Indicators

That is our background. Now I hope a brief review of a few indicators covering twelve-month periods immediately "before" and "after" will stimulate you to examine our ten-year experience thoroughly.*

	UP	DOWN
Laundry Manhours		4.5%
Laundry Volume	13.9%	
Laundry Supplies		27.8%
Average Laundry Salary	18.5%	
Housekeeping Manhours		11.1%
Housekeeping Supplies		12.9%
Average Housekeeping Salary	15.2%	
Laboratory Manhours		4.6%
Laboratory Supplies		3.3%
Laboratory Procedures	3.2%	
Average Laboratory Salary	9.3%	
Nursing Manhours		6.0%
Linen Replacement and Loss		56.5%
Nursing Supplies		7.1%
Average Nursing Salary	11.2%	
Radiology Manhours		5.4%
Radiology Supplies		8.6%

*Details in Appendix D

	UP	DOWN
Radiology Procedures		1.8%
Average Radiology Salary	12.1%	
Dietary Manhours		2.4%
Food	3.0%	
Dietary Supplies		24.2%
Meals	1.4%	
Average Dietary Salary	10.3%	
Electrodiagnostic Manhours		18.1%
Electrodiagnostic Supplies		.3%
Electrodiagnostic Procedures		.4%
Average Electrodiagnostic Salary	28.6%	
Medical Records Manhours		11.1%
Medical Records Supplies		18.8%
Average Medical Records Salary	18.2%	

During the writing of our first draft, we had thought to call this book *How To Save A Billion Dollars*. We dropped the Madison Avenue title because we were afraid it might turn off some conservative doubting Thomases. But—if hospitals of size embark on such methods, who knows how large the collective savings may be, not once, but indefinitely?

BEFORES AND AFTERS

The following "before" and "after" comparisons demonstrate the improvement experienced with the introduction of productivity incentive plans. In each instance the twelve-month periods immediately preceding and following implementation are presented. It is the sum of these improvements and the continued relative progress in subsequent years that contributed so significantly to the results depicted throughout this book.

Nursing

The Productivity Incentive Program in Nursing went into effect in May of 1965. Although all indicators reflected good results, the rather dramatic drop in linen costs was particularly significant. This and the subsequent year's experience (1967–68 fiscal year reported $15,636 in linen replacement cost) supported the contention that Nursing could control linen loss.

Table B-1 Nursing	1965-66	1966-67
	(12 Months Before)	(12 Months After)
Average Census	269	267
Average Paid Hours Per Pay Period	27,385	26,696
Excluding INU & ICCU	26,835	25,232
Linen Replacement	$ 24,724	$ 10,767
Supplies	$120,277	$111,681
Drugs	$168,668	$156,006

Laboratory

In August 1966 a formula was implemented in the General Laboratory. The experience in this department followed that of earlier applications.

Table B-2 Laboratory	1965-1966	1966-67
	(12 Months Before)	(12 Months After)
Procedures	164,131	169,434
Manhours	54,189	51,705
Salaries	$121,748	$126,991
Supplies*	$ 44,104	$ 42,637
Cost Per Procedure	$1.01	$1.00

* The supply expense as shown, includes certain procedures performed in outside laboratories. The inconsistencies among hospitals in counting laboratory procedures lead to a wide variation in HAS reports. This makes these and other laboratory comparisons between hospitals quite difficult.

Laundry

In 1964, Laundry productivity averaged forty-two pounds of linen per manhour. With a 10 percent increase in capacity, a comparable volume increase was achieved with reduced manhours, achieving an almost immediate 20 percent productivity increase as reflected below.

Table B-3 Laundry

	1964	1965
	(12 Months Before)	(12 Months After)
Pounds of Linen	1,372,565	1,563,819
Manhours	25,897	24,738
Salaries	$32,177	$35,662
Supplies	$11,121	$ 8,027
Pay Per Hour	$1.24	$1.47
Cost Per Pound	3.15¢	2.79¢

Surgery

Ironically, no productivity element was included in the original plan for Surgery. This superior department was 25 to 30 percent above HAS medians in what was felt to be a rather sophisticated surgical environment for a 325-bed hospital. The goal was supply cost reduction, and its 5 to 10 percent improvement set the stage for similar experience in the professional departments which followed.

Table B-4 Surgery

	1964	1965
	(12 Months Before)	(12 Months After)
Operations	7,969	8,055
Salaries	$112,881	$136,458
Supplies	$ 91,734	$ 85,522

Housekeeping

A plan was placed into operation in the Housekeeping Department January 1, 1966. A concerted effort on supply reduction in 1965 had already created a saving of $5,756 the previous year. Thus, 1966 supply savings were $8,711 below 1964, or approximately 30 percent.

Table B-5 Housekeeping

	Fiscal Years	
	1965	1966
Manhours	110,885	98,565
Salaries	$124,663	$127,265
Supplies	$ 22,984	$ 20,029
Pay Per Manhour	$1.12	$1.29

Radiology

The Productivity Incentive Plan in Radiology was initiated January 1, 1966. Note that the number of x rays dropped from the previous calendar year, thus making it more difficult to achieve productivity increases and supply savings.

Table B-6 Radiology

	1965 (Calendar Year Before)	1966 (Calendar Year After)
Procedures	24,598	23,496
Manhours	27,540	26,063
Salaries	$62,578	$58,960
Supplies	$53,998	$49,332
Cost per x ray	$4.74	$4.61

Dietary

A Productivity Incentive Plan was introduced into Dietary in 1966. The short term experience does not permit a full evaluation. However, the two prime factors in the formula were manhours and nonfood supply costs, and there was a stabilization of these costs consistent with results in other departments.

Table B-7 Dietary

	Fiscal Years	
	1965	1966
Meals	369,346	359,087
Manhours	123,909	121,319
Salaries	$133,525	$141,497
Supplies	$ 40,445	$ 41,588
Food	$128,994	$130,023
Pay Per Manhour	$1.08	$1.17

	Fiscal Years	
	1967	1968
Meals	364,285	370,116
Manhours	120,828	118,521
Salaries	$155,591	$183,577
Supplies	$ 31,582	$ 24,850
Food	$134,736	$143,088
Pay Per Manhour	$1.29	$1.54

Electrodiagnostics

In early 1966, pulmonary function studies were transferred from this department to the newly created Pulmonary Laboratory. This resulted in a decline in procedures, creating, as in Radiology, a difficult situation in which to improve productivity. Nonetheless, productivity did improve from 0.85 procedures per manhour to 0.99 procedures per manhour—1.65 percent.

Table B-8 Electrodiagnostics

	June 1965–May 1966 (12 Months Before)	June 1966–May 1967 (12 Months After)
Procedures	7,626	7,289
Manhours	8,996	7,366
Salaries	$12,622	$13,233
Supplies	$ 5,067	$ 4,905
Cost Per Procedure	$2.32	$2.49
Pay Per Hour	$1.40	$1.80

Medical Records

Medical Records began its Productivity Incentive Program on April 1, 1967. A new and improved central dictation system had been installed in 1966, which led to a substantial increase in dictation. The three fiscal years covering these events are depicted below.

Table B-9 Medical Records

	Fiscal Year		
	1965–66	1966–67	1967–68
Paid Manhours	19,492	18,791	16,648
Salaries	$36,645	$38,276	$40,012
Supplies	$12,105	$13,459	$10,921
Salary Per Manhour	$1.88	$2.03	$2.40

Appendix C

Baptist Hospital Financial Indicators

Table C-1 Baptist Hospital Base Data: Annual Audits

Year	Operating Expenses	Payroll Expenses	Patient Days	Admissions	Employees - FTE
1963	$ 2,800,176	$1,748,688	88,592	15,017	562
1964	3,109,267	1,975,233	93,073	15,403	591
1965	3,556,643	2,255,466	98,488	16,152	620
1966	4,140,412	2,522,666	97,544	15,508	607
1967	4,425,311	2,786,901	97,014	14,856	617
1968	5,071,835	3,274,490	98,371	14,891	637
1969	6,212,566	3,879,928	114,015	15,142	729
1970	7,345,987	4,596,919	120,328	15,338	772
1971	8,634,444	5,149,526	122,799	16,278	799
1972	9,555,646	5,691,067	131,757	17,047	854
1973	10,877,479	6,501,827	142,842	17,703	977
1974	12,837,828	7,645,314	154,442	19,682	1,093

The above data in Table C-1 are taken from the annual audits of Baptist Hospital and manhour reports for the last pay period of each fiscal year. These base data are utilized for many tables and comparisons that follow. Please note the following:

- Years are fiscal years ending September 30. Thus, 1963 is 10/1/62 through 9/30/63.
- 1963 and 1964 are "preproductivity incentive years." In 1964, preparations were in progress for a new addition opened in the fall of that year.
- 1965 was the first year of the productivity incentive program.
- In 1968 and 1969, most contract physicians began separate billing. This results in a lower patient cost, and Baptist's per day and per admission costs should be qualified accordingly.

117

- On January 1, 1969, Baptist Hospital acquired its Specialty Care Center located across the street from the central facility. This facility houses mental health, alcoholic intervention, and extended care. While nursing manhours are high on these units, it should be noted that (1) per diem costs are lower than usual because of the absence of many high cost ancillary services, (2) per admission costs are higher because of longer stays, and (3) overall expense in the operation of this facility is less because of its "satellite" nature, relatively low acquisition cost, and depreciation and certain economies of scale realized.
- In January of 1971, approximately forty new beds were opened as part of a construction program begun in 1969 and completed in April 1972.
- In 1972, an additional fifty beds were added upon completion of construction.

Table C-2 Costs Per Patient Day

Year	Baptist	Florida*	Difference	U.S.*	Difference
1963	$31.61	$ 39.16	$ 7.55	$ 39.87	$ 8.26
1964	33.41	41.48	8.07	42.47	9.06
1965	36.11	44.11	8.00	45.40	9.29
1966	42.45	47.98	5.53	48.94	6.49
1967	45.62	53.69	8.07	54.99	9.37
1968	51.56	60.11	8.55	62.18	10.62
1969	54.49	67.77	13.28	71.07	16.58
1970	61.05	78.51	17.46	81.80	20.75
1971	70.31	91.20	20.89	93.84	23.53
1972	72.52	99.82	27.30	105.13	32.61
1973	76.15	110.16	34.01	114.43	38.25
1974	83.12	129.37	46.25	127.33	44.31

* *Source:* AHA Guide Issues—nongovernment, not-for-profit, short term general and other special hospitals.

Table C-2 and Figure C-1 indicate a slower rate of increase in costs per patient day for Baptist Hospital since implementation of productivity incentive plans. The disparity is not as great as indicated because of the qualifications cited under the table on Baptist Hospital Base Data with respect to separate professional bill and Specialty Care Center. Furthermore, Baptist enjoyed a steady annual volume increase beginning in 1969, which promotes increased productivity and cost control.

Figure C-1

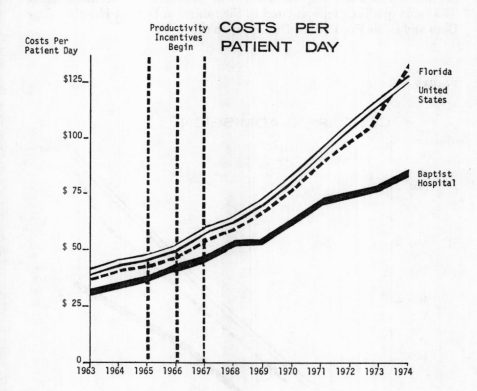

Table C-3 Costs Per Admission

Year	Baptist	Florida*	Difference	U.S.*	Difference
1963	$186	$270	$ 84	$ 303	$117
1964	202	286	84	324	122
1965	220	304	84	350	130
1966	267	350	83	386	119
1967	298	412	114	452	154
1968	341	481	140	525	184
1969	410	550	140	597	187
1970	479	614	135	676	197
1971	530	693	163	760	230
1972	561	747	186	840	279
1973	614	815	201	908	294
1974	652	979	327	1,005	353

* *Source:* AHA Guide Issues—nongovernmental, nonprofit, short term general and other special hospitals.

Table C-3 and Figure C-2 indicate a slower rate of increase in costs per admission since implementation of productivity incentive plans. The same qualifications as cited in the tables on Baptist Hospital Base Data and Costs Per Patient Day apply to this table.

Figure C-2

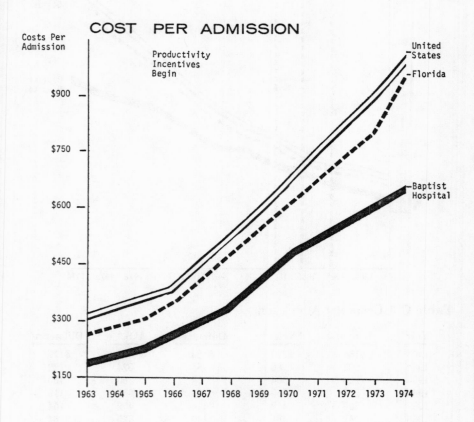

The productivity incentive program can be solely credited with raising salaries of Baptist Hospital personnel from below state and national levels prior to 1965 to above in the years to follow. The decline in recent years can be attributed to (1) substantial staff increases of short tenure personnel as patient volume expanded, and (2) the status quo of the productivity incentive program forced by the IRS issue referred to in the main text.

Table C-4 Average Annual Salary

Year	Baptist	Florida*	Difference	U.S.*	Difference
1963	$3,111	$3,167	$- 56	$3,667	$- 556
1964	3,342	3,402	- 60	3,861	- 519
1965	3,638	3,511	+128	4,044	- 406
1966	4,156	3,659	+497	4,113	+ 43
1967	4,517	4,152	+365	4,510	+ 7
1968	5,140	4,479	+661	4,937	+203
1969	5,322	4,984	+338	5,396	- 74
1970	5,955	5,536	+419	6,013	- 58
1971	6,445	6,156	+389	6,629	- 184
1972	6,664	6,402	+262	7,119	- 455
1973	6,655	6,586	+ 69	7,454	- 799
1974	6,995	7,249	- 254	7,865	- 870

* *Source:* AHA Guide Issues—nongovernmental, nonprofit, short term general and other special hospitals.

Figure C-3

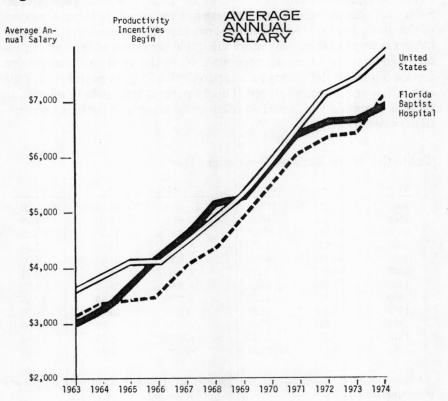

Table C-5 Payroll as a Percent of Total Expense

Year	Baptist	Florida*	Difference	U.S.*	Difference
1963	51%	56%	- 5%	62%	- 11%
1964	58%	55%	+ 3%	62%	- 4%
1965	62%	57%	+ 5%	62%	—
1966	65%	55%	+10%	61%	+ 4%
1967	63%	56%	+ 7%	60%	+ 3%
1968	65%	56%	+ 9%	60%	+ 5%
1969	62%	55%	+ 7%	59%	+ 3%
1970	63%	56%	+ 7%	59%	+ 4%
1971	60%	55%	+ 5%	58%	+ 2%
1972	60%	53%	+ 7%	57%	+ 3%
1973	60%	52%	+ 8%	56%	+ 4%
1974	60%	51%	+ 9%	55%	+ 5%

* *Source:* Nongovernmental, nonprofit, short term, general and other special hospitals.

This companion table (Table C-5) to Table C-4—Average Annual Salary reflects the significant increase in employee salaries as a percent of the operating expense dollar (and consequent decrease in supply and other expense) that accompanied the implementation of Baptist Hospital's productivity incentive programs. Note the relative improvement from a 5 percent deficiency as compared with Florida hospitals in 1963 and a 10 percent excess in 1966. This 15 percent total gain in relation to Florida hospitals was matched identically when compared to the national category.

Table C-6 Other Expense Per Patient Day

Year	Baptist	Florida*	Difference	U.S.*	Difference
1963	$11.87	$17.44	$- 5.57	$15.36	$- 3.39
1964	12.18	18.51	- 6.33	16.33	- 4.15
1965	13.21	19.01	- 5.80	17.46	- 4.25
1966	16.58	21.68	- 5.10	18.97	- 2.39
1967	16.89	23.70	- 6.71	21.89	- 5.00
1968	18.27	26.32	- 8.05	25.04	- 6.77
1969	20.46	30.36	- 9.90	29.04	- 8.58
1970	22.85	34.91	-12.06	33.65	-10.80
1971	28.38	41.31	-12.97	39.13	-10.75
1972	29.33	47.08	-17.75	45.22	-15.89
1973	30.63	53.18	-22.55	50.29	-19.66
1974	33.62	63.51	-29.89	57.55	-23.93

* *Source:* AHA Guide Issue—nongovernmental, not-for-profit, short term general and other special hospitals.

In the preface it was noted that Baptist Hospital "had to scratch hard for financial integrity" from the date of its opening in 1951. Hence, supplies and other expenses traditionally were kept under relatively tight control. In addition to this traditional element, we believe the following have been key contributors to these results:

- The productivity incentive programs. Please note that other expense during the program's developing years (1966–1969) increased only $3.88 per day at Baptist, while hospitals in Florida increased $8.68, and U.S. hospitals experienced a $10.07 climb. From these base years, the disparity continued to grow.
- Lower expenses for construction, land acquisition, utilities, and some other supplies and services.

Figure C-4

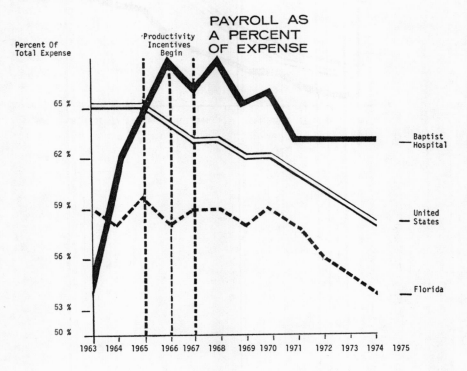

Figure C-5

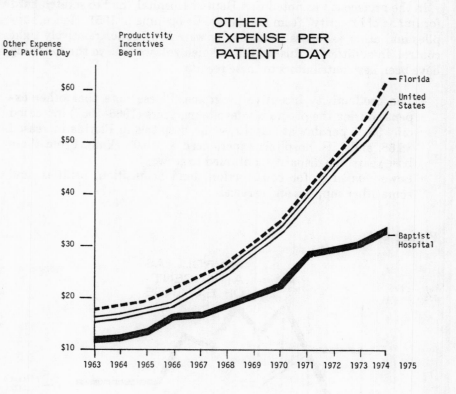

Hospital Administrative Services Productivity Indicators

GENERAL OBSERVATIONS

The indicators used in the following comparisons cover the three-month periods ending with September, the closing of each respective fiscal year for Baptist Hospital. Thus, fluctuations exist that might be reflected in these statistics. The other options would be (1) the use of monthly indicators, which would have great fluctuation; or (2) calculate annual data, which would be interpolation on the part of the author and qualify, perhaps, the authenticity of the source. Nonetheless, the HAS indicators reflect accurately the productivity gains experienced by Baptist Hospital as a result of its productivity incentive program.

Some departments are not included in HAS data for various reasons. An example is Electrodiagnostics (Electrocardiography, Electroencephalography, Ultrasound, etc.), which is a sophisticated and productive department at Baptist. Application of the productivity incentive concept in this department, combined with effective departmental leadership, resulted in significant gains in output and higher performance standards. Unfortunately, state and national comparisons are not available. Another department not included that reflects similar sophistication and productivity gains includes Pulmonary Services.

It is interesting to note the experience in Pharmacy. As described in the text, Pharmacy was included as a part of the nursing formula. Though the more direct incentive was absent, the unique drug administration system in effect for twenty years and modified by Brewer system equipment in 1963–64 has enabled Baptist to maintain an unusually high performance in the absence of a unit system for this department.

Note the several qualifications referred to in the tables. HAS data are an unusually valuable reference source for hospitals; but, despite their best efforts, reporting is occasionally inconsistent with guidelines.

Table D-1 Laundry Productivity*

Year	Baptist	Florida	Difference	National	Difference
1963	45.74			35.88	9.86
1964	39.68			34.54	5.14
1965	47.77			31.72	16.05
1966	50.42			31.11	19.31
1967	47.49			32.86	14.63
1968	45.67			33.98	11.69
1969	56.48			36.44	20.04
1970	67.52	40.29	27.23	38.28	29.24
1971	64.05	43.93	20.12	42.67	21.38
1972	66.49	49.53	16.96	43.30	23.19
1973	73.52	46.15	27.17	45.89	27.63
1974	73.85	48.44	25.41	45.44	28.41

* Pounds per manhour is the indicator

In the two years prior to the introduction of the productivity incentive program in this department, it averaged 21 percent higher pounds per manhour than the national category performance. With the increased volume occasioned by the expansion of late 1964 and, in our opinion, the sole motivational force of the new incentive program, productivity jumps to 50 percent over the national average. With still greater volume the next year, it was 60 percent greater than the national indicator.

The introduction of percale sheets with their lighter weight affected the pounds per manhour index, and accounted for the paper decline for Baptist Hospital in 1967 and 1968.

Table D-2 Laboratory Productivity*

Year	Baptist	Florida	Difference	National	Difference
1963	3.85			3.25	0.60
1964	3.28			3.11	0.17
1965	4.35			2.99	1.36
1966	4.60			3.20	1.40
1967	5.48			3.31	2.17
1968	4.96			3.28	1.68
1969	4.93			3.50	1.43
1970	8.04	4.05	3.99	3.81	4.23
1971	9.36	4.17	5.19	4.14	5.22
1972	7.99	4.69	3.30	4.16	3.83
1973	14.02	6.58	7.44	5.12	8.90
1974	13.80	6.86	6.94	5.47	8.33

* Procedures per manhour is the indicator

Figure D-1

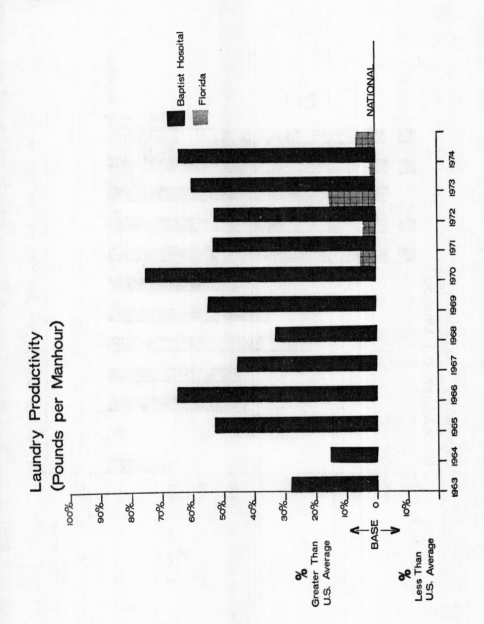

Figure D-2

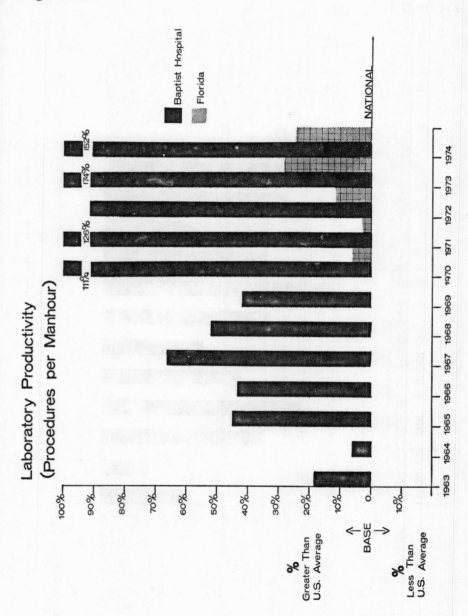

With the implementation of an incentive program in Laboratory, productivity increased over 30 percent in one year's span, though the approximate 15 percent reflected from 1963–65 could be a more accurate indication. Later, productivity gains should be attributed more to automation than to the merits of productivity incentives.

In recent years, methods of counting laboratory procedures and progress in automation appear to have qualified the reliability of the HAS indicators.

Table D-3 Surgery Productivity*

Year	Baptist	Florida	Difference	National	Difference
1963	6.57			9.64	3.07
1964	7.48			9.50	2.02
1965	8.17			10.05	1.88
1966	8.88			9.76	0.88
1967	8.96			10.93	1.97
1968	9.68			11.46	1.88
1969	8.58			10.17	1.69
1970	7.84	11.21	3.37	10.40	2.56
1971	8.35	10.06	1.71	10.22	1.87
1972	8.24	10.55	2.31	10.26	2.02
1973	8.31	11.44	3.13	10.47	2.16
1974	9.25	11.23	1.98	10.58	1.33

* 1963–1968—Manhours per operation is the indicator.
  1969 to date—Manhours per visit is the indicator.

As noted in the text, a productivity factor was not included in the formula for surgery because the departmental leadership has always been productivity minded. HAS indicators over the years have reflected productivity of 25 percent above average in this department with, it is felt, above average sophistication for hospitals of comparable size.

Table D-4 Nursing Productivity*

Year	Baptist	Florida	Difference	National	Difference
1963	5.63			6.06	0.43
1964	5.92			5.58	(0.34)
1965	5.65			5.64	(0.01)
1966	5.78			5.58	(0.20)

* 1963–1969—Manhours per patient day is the indicator.
  1970 to date—Manhours per patient date for medical and surgical units is the indicator.

Figure D-3

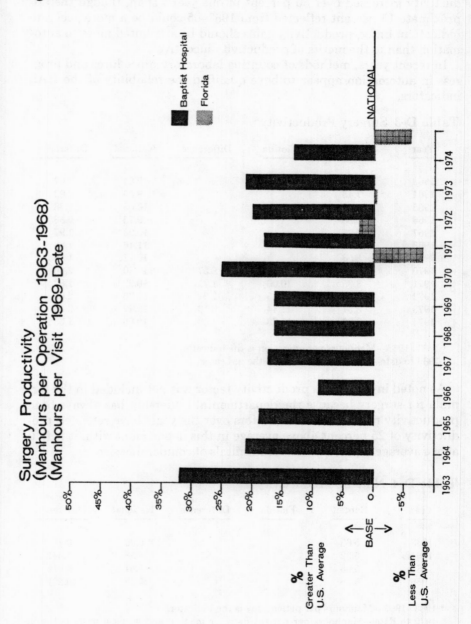

Table D-4 Nursing Productivity* (Cont.)

Year	Baptist	Florida	Difference	National	Difference
1967	5.52			5.68	0.16
1968	5.86			6.01	0.15
1969	5.13			5.62	0.49
1970	5.17	5.94	0.77	5.88	0.71
1971	5.68	6.32	0.64	6.06	0.38
1972	5.32	6.91	1.59	6.00	0.68
1973	5.39	6.09	0.70	5.58	0.19
1974	5.12	7.10	1.98	5.52	0.40

The "before–after" table reflects better the productivity gains achieved by nursing with the implementation of productivity incentives. During the period of implementation, Baptist Hospital introduced the concepts of intensive coronary care and surgical intensive nursing units to this area. The additional staffing for these units was accomplished within the total context of slightly reduced manhours from the initial year (1966) through 1969.

Table D-5 Radiology Productivity*

Year	Baptist	Florida	Difference	National	Difference
1963	1.08			0.80	0.28
1964	0.84			0.87	(0.03)
1965	0.87			0.75	0.12
1966	0.88			0.73	0.15
1967	0.91			0.75	0.16
1968	0.89			0.78	0.11
1969	0.91			1.27	0.36
1970	0.99	1.48	0.49	1.31	0.32
1971	0.96	1.48	0.52	1.36	0.40
1972	0.89	1.46	0.57	1.34	0.45
1973	1.10	1.41	0.31	1.33	0.23
1974	0.98	1.43	0.45	1.30	0.32

* 1963–1968—Procedures per manhour is the indicator.
1969 to date—Manhours per procedure is the indicator.

Although earlier the Radiology Department was quite productive, the year before productivity incentives were started at Baptist Hospital its effectiveness was below national averages. (During these years one will remember that there was little change in this service from year to year. The great technological advances that have marked the past decade were just beginning.) With the introduction of a productivity incentive

Figure D-4

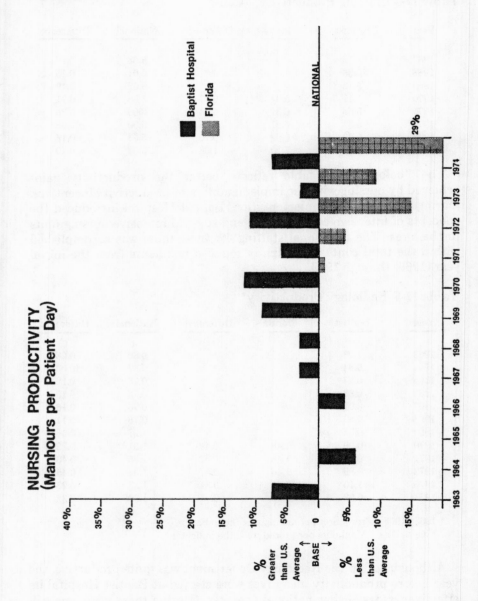

Figure D-5

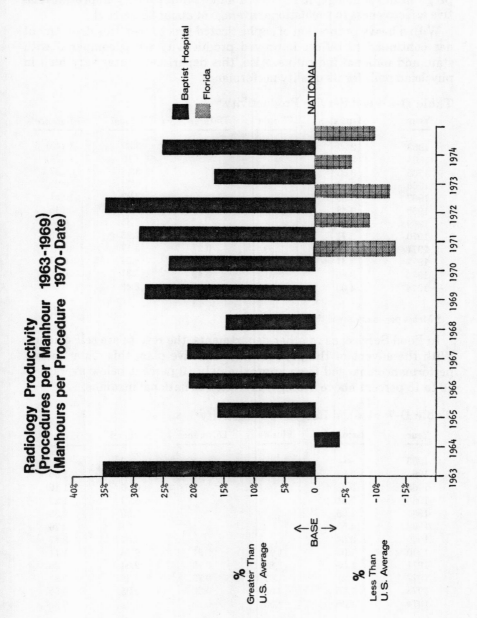

program in Radiology, it registered almost immediately improved relative effectiveness to the national average of about 20 percent.

With a heavy proportion of sophisticated procedures, this department has continued to reflect improved productivity when compared with state and national indicators. Also, this department rates very high in physician polls for its quality performance.

Table D-6 Food Service Productivity*

Year	Baptist	Florida	Difference	National	Difference
1963	2.96			3.39	(0.43)
1964	2.86			3.10	(0.24)
1965	3.55			3.18	0.37
1966	3.38			3.09	0.29
1967	3.50			2.99	0.51
1968	3.48			3.00	0.48
1969	3.95			3.35	0.60
1970	3.74	3.07	0.67	2.95	0.79
1971	3.16	2.89	0.27	3.17	(0.01)
1972	3.81	2.90	0.91	3.24	0.67
1973	3.80	3.31	0.49	3.31	0.49
1974	4.02	3.45	0.57	3.43	0.59

* Meals per manhour is the indicator.

In Food Service, as in other departments, the results are self-evident. With the advent of the productivity incentive plan, this department's performance changed from approximately 10 percent below average to 10 to 15 percent above average, as related to national medians.

Table D-7 Medical Records Productivity*

Year	Baptist	Florida	Difference	National	Difference
1963	—			—	—
1964	3.85			6.73	2.88
1965	5.28			6.40	1.12
1966	5.51			6.73	1.22
1967	4.95			7.30	2.35
1968	4.55			7.31	2.76
1969	3.84			7.31	3.47
1970	1.05	1.92	0.87	2.16	1.11
1971	1.08	1.87	0.79	2.04	0.96
1972	1.21	1.87	0.76	2.12	0.91
1973	1.15	2.05	0.90	2.05	0.90
1974	1.36	2.05	0.69	2.22	0.86

* 1964–1969—Manhours per bed is the indicator.
1970 to date—Manhours per discharge unit is the indicator.

Figure D-6

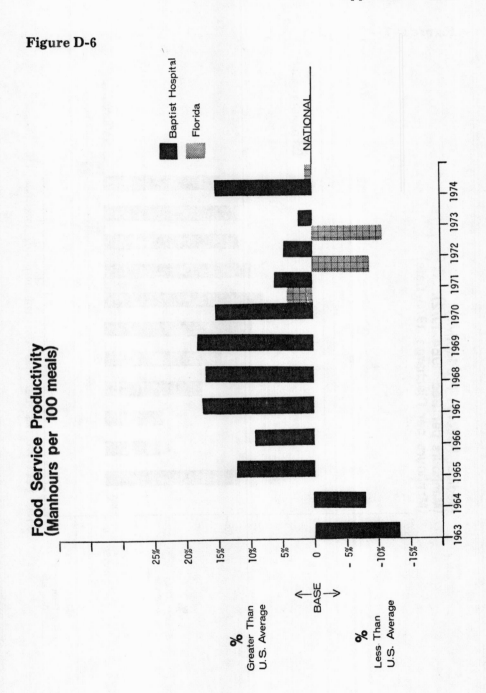

Figure D-7

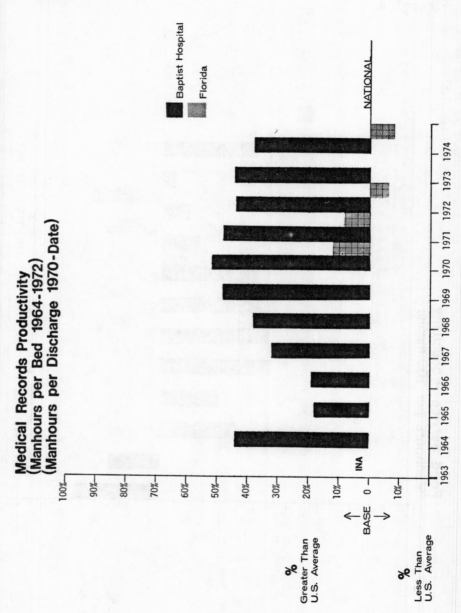

Medical Records Productivity
(Manhours per Bed 1964-1972)
(Manhours per Discharge 1970-Date)

This department (among others) is a classic example of the gains that can be achieved when the department head is productivity-oriented. Baptist was among the early hospitals to install complete dictating services along with other services to facilitate the physicians' work. (The disparity between Baptist's 1964 and 1965 indicators reflects introduction of centralized dictation service and physical expansion.) During the period the productivity incentive system was installed, the unique application for medical stenographers devised by the department head led to almost immediate and dramatic gains for this unit. This type of leadership and the productivity incentive program for this department led to the gains first experienced in 1966 and 1967, which continue through the present.

Table D-8 Pharmacy Productivity*

Year	Baptist	Florida	Difference	National	Difference
1963	—			—	—
1964	1.10			2.83	1.73
1965	1.93			2.92	0.99
1966	1.79			3.09	1.30
1967	1.91			3.23	1.32
1968	1.97			3.38	1.41
1969	17.48			10.22	7.26
1970	22.40	10.58	11.82	10.97	11.43
1971	24.89	15.24	9.65	10.92	13.97
1972	17.52	10.38	7.14	10.74	6.78
1973	18.42	9.79	8.63	10.94	7.48
1974	17.47	9.88	7.59	10.54	6.93

* 1964–1968—Manhours per bed is the indicator.
  1969 to date—Line items per manhour is the indicator.

Credit for Pharmacy's high productivity goes to the Central Drug Administration system established in 1953 more so than the productivity incentive program. The Central Drug System was very effective productivitywise and qualitywise, reducing Pharmacy and Nursing manhours while simultaneously reducing drug incidents. It was installed in a 140-bed hospital and, by the early 1960s, had become inadequate for a 300-bed hospital. The Brewer System introduced in the early 1960s provided mechanical and automated support, which has enabled the Central Drug Administration to continue to the present time. However, a change to a unit dose system will likely be made in the near future.

As described in the text, Pharmacy was a part of the nursing productivity formula inasmuch as these functions were so closely intertwined.

Figure D-8

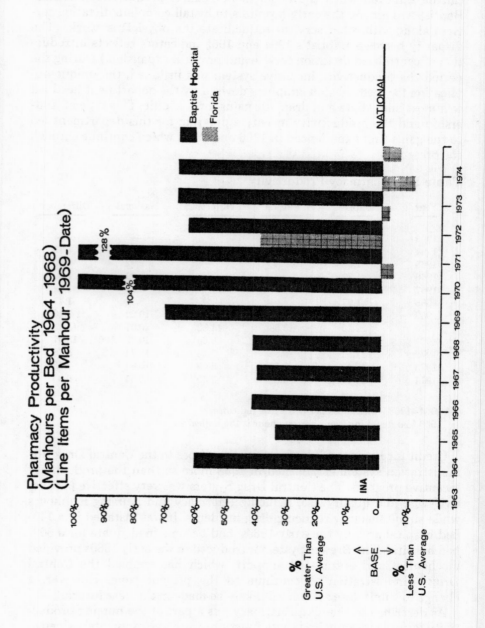

Index

About the Author

Pat N. Groner is Executive Director of Baptist Hospital, Pensacola, Florida, and a widely recognized leader in the field of cost containment. He is past president of the Florida Hospital Association and Southeastern Hospital Conference and is currently Vice-Chairman, American Hospital Association Special Committee on the Regulatory Process. He is widely published in the field of hospital administration.